Super Omnia Bonae Voluntatis

Reflections
of an
Uncommon
Monk

Reflections of an Uncommon Monk

Toward a Theology of Hero-Sainthood

Brother Emmanuel Labrise, O.S.B.

A Hero Is Chosen

Book One

Saint Joseph Books

Table of Contents

Introduction to the Series

Reflections of an Uncommon Monk is the first book in the A Hero Is Chosen series and serves as its spiritual and moral foundation. Beginning with the second book, *Mission of the Maiden*, all of the stories build on the topics and themes introduced in *Reflections of an Uncommon Monk*. The primary aim of this series is to transmit Christian spiritual principles and to teach moral virtue in the context of a hero-saint story.

A note here should be made on the central concept and predominant themes in each book beginning with *Mission of the Maiden*. Each story, whether historical or fictional, tells the tale of one or more hero-saints called by God to a particular vocation and chosen by him to fulfill a personal mission. Historical context is crucial. A large portion of each book is dedicated to placing the protagonist within his or her historical setting in which he or she is offered an opportunity to perform a task or set of tasks, and endure an event or set of events, that qualifies him or her for hero-sainthood. In all cases except Remmy Kimm, who appears in the fiction tale, *A Vocation Story Never Told*, this occurs during the latter part of their lives, sometimes lasting years or as little as one day.

The timeframe is less important than the hero-event or hero-moment itself. One may become a hero-saint through a single heroic act at the end of one's life or through a lifetime of unselfish service. Dom Tom Mo, the other protagonist in *A Vocation Story Never Told*, was called to sacrifice his life for the passengers aboard his spacecraft within the span of a few hours. Remmy Kimm, on the other hand, was called to years of missionary service and to survive a near-death experience. Both are martyrs, one red (blood, death) and the other white (selfless service to others).

Also less important than the hero-event and hero-moment is the station in life one occupies when he or she is called. Joan of Arc was called out of obscurity to a public mission lasting less than a year and culminated in her being burned at the stake as a heretic. Thomas More was called out of prominence to sacrifice his high standing in English society and even his life for loyalty to the faith he had professed. Jesus of Nazareth was also called out of obscurity to a public ministry lasting about three years and ending with his crucifixion. The hero-event and hero-moment also eclipse whatever competencies or assets one possesses when called. With the possible exception of Saint Thomas More, all are underdog stories.

A second note should be made on where these books fit within the realm of literature. In my opinion, none of the books in this series, whether historical or fictional, is in the strict sense a work of biography, history, or fiction, even if they contain biographical accounts, historical content, or fiction. Much less are they hagiographies, even if they deal with the lives of canonized saints. They are instead hero-saint stories existing within the genre of nonfiction Christian literature.

Those who appreciate the work of Joseph Campbell, especially his highly influential *The Hero with a Thousand Faces*, might find something worthwhile in the pages of these books. I have not attempted to model the fictional characters on his writing, however, nor have I attempted to frame the retelling of these stories of actual historical persons based on his work on myth and mythical figures. It is more that I am attracted to the archetype and archetypical behavior of the hero-saint that lies deep within the unconscious of every human person, at least if you subscribe to Jungian theory. This archetype, like so many others, manifests itself in movies, books, art, and public performances of every age from antiquity to the popular films of today. It is the archetype of the hero-saint that serves as the psychological foundation for the stories in this series.

I thought it helpful to provide a brief lexicon of terms on which the reader may focus. I cannot provide definitions for each, however, as there is a certain fluidity of meaning depending on a person's life, but at least the mention of them will help to make the reader aware of the important aspects of each story and the subject matter and flavor of this series. The lexicon appears on the following page.

A Lexicon of Terms

1. Capstone experience
2. Death-leading-unto-eternity
3. Desert experience
4. Deus ex machina
5. Fulfillment in life
6. Hero quest
7. Hero story
8. Hero-adventure
9. Hero-event
10. Hero-moment
11. Hero-saint
12. Life journey
13. Meaning in life
14. Mission
15. Mission sequence
16. Mystery
17. Oceans of eternity
18. Personal holiness
19. Pilgrim
20. Pilgrimage
21. Purification
22. Purpose in life
23. Reward
24. Sainthood
25. Saint-in-the-making
26. Sanctification
27. Sands of time
28. Satisfaction in life
29. Tides of history
30. Value in life
31. Vocation
32. Wayfarer
33. Winds of change

Book One

Reflections of an Uncommon Monk

Introduction to Book One

Every book is something of a journey, and the journey you will take through this humble, little book stands as a metaphor for the journey we all take through life. *Reflections of an Uncommon Monk* is about life and death, pilgrimage and quest, destiny, destination, and eternity.

The journey of this book begins on the front cover. Its artwork serves as a visual representation or snapshot of that journey. Just as stained glass windows in a church are designed to teach and tell a story, the symbolism in the cover's artwork sums up the content of this book and is meant to convey a message. The upper portion of the desert sky at nightfall points toward the future and the universe, which is itself a symbol of eternity, and connects with the first reflection, "It Begins with a Dream." Dreams are a first step toward the fulfillment of something that lies in the future. All dreams look forward, upward, outward, and beyond. They look toward the future, and in a very real sense toward eternity, for the future is eternal, and eternity is the future for all of us. This book begins with a dream.

The lower portion of the cover artwork features the earth on which we walk and journey through life. The monk is you and me, and the journey he or she takes through the desert represents your journey and mine through life. The horizon toward which the monk travels has both an earthly, temporal element and an eternal, celestial element. All of us journey toward that horizon, willingly or unwillingly. Our dreams and how we live our lives on earth will help shape our final destination and how we will spend eternity, but the most important aspect of this mystery is what God wills for us. It is a fundamental spiritual truth that you always get what you want when it comes to God, but we should also ask ourselves if God always gets what he wants when it comes to us.

Our journey through life, like our journey through this book, whether we admit it or not, is essentially solitary yet at the same time communal. The aloneness of the desert, a place sought out by monks from the origins of monasticism, Christian or otherwise, may be a *place* like the Sahara or the Judean desert, but it is always a *state* of prayer, contemplation, and proximity to God. The final illustration following the Afterword represents the ambiguous fulfillment of the monk's journey and ours as the footprints disappear into the vast deserts of time and distant horizons of the future and eternity. We do not know how the monk's journey unfolded or where his path led him, but we know his or her journey was purposeful, and that we are also on a journey, purposeful or not.

This book begins with a dream and ends in eternity. It is a journey whose path is one of discipleship that culminates in personal holiness, and the footprints in the final illustration represent the way of those who walk it. For a chosen few, the path is one of audacious discipleship that leads to hero-sainthood.

Reflections of an Uncommon Monk is composed of twenty-seven spiritual reflections that serve as a moral and spiritual foundation for the hero stories in this series. Sometimes the connection between the spiritual or moral truth and the historical or fictional account is overt, as with the chapter headings that refer back to an element in the reflection, "A Hero Is Chosen." Mostly the connection is implied, as with the reflection, "The Fullness of Time," which is universal throughout these books. The diligent reader will profit most if he or she would read the stories in light of the reflections. It should not be too difficult of an exercise and would be well worth the effort.

Included in the back of this book are a number of blank pages set aside for notes. If you come across something particularly meaningful to you, please make a note of the page number and any thoughts you consider worth remembering. At the end of your journey, you might review those notes as an additional means for personal growth. Please regard it as something of a journal.

For, although we are in the flesh, we do not battle according to the flesh, for the weapons of our battle are not of flesh but are enormously powerful, capable of destroying fortresses. We destroy arguments and every pretension raising itself against the knowledge of God, and take every thought captive in obedience to Christ.

2 Corinthians 10:3–5

1

It Begins with a Dream

I have heard it said that there are gifts we will *surely* receive from God whether we pray for them or not, there are gifts we will *never* receive from God whether we pray for them or not, and there are gifts we will *only* receive from God if we pray for them.

It begins with a dream.

Then comes prayer.

Then hope.

~

We all have dreams, little and great. Yet there are times in the lives of some of us when one dream rises above the rest, one all-encompassing thought or vision that gives meaning to one's life and serves as a kind of central, organizing principle. Some dreams change the world.

Martin Luther King had a dream. "I have a dream…," he said and prayed. He loved his dream so much that he was willing to die for it. I have often thought that the character of a person is measured by what he or she is willing to sacrifice for what he or she most values. Some dreams are that valuable. Some dreams are worth dying for.

I do not know if Henry Ford prayed, but I know he had a dream. He recognized the life-changing benefits the newly invented automobile could bring to individual Americans and the nation as a whole, and he imagined that he could devise a way to mass-produce a highly durable and easily maintained automobile he could sell at an affordable price. The historian Paul Johnson wrote of Ford: "He illustrated the power, which all historians learn to recognize, of a good but simple idea pursued single-mindedly, by a man of implacable will." There is nothing perfect in this world and industrialization has come at a cost, but there is no question that motorized vehicles have improved the quality of life for billions of people. Some dreams are worth living for, and some people live to see their dreams come true.

Dreams can be powerful, and some can be painful and dangerous. It is wise to be careful when it comes to dreams and wishes. Some dreams have eternal consequences. An old monk once taught me that we always get what we want when it comes to God. He was not referring to superficial, transitory desires that involve some temporal gain without reference to our spiritual good. He was instead referring to those desires that lie deep within our hearts, the ones that survive into eternity. The ancient Greeks left us a great piece of advice: "Know thyself," and the only way to truly know thyself is to spend quality time on a regular basis in silence and solitude in deep self-reflection and meditation. Scripture teaches how torturous the human heart is (Jeremiah 17:9). Know thyself! What we do not know can hurt us.

Dreams can also be costly and sometimes futile. There is a Junkyard of Broken Dreams in the annals of human history filled with stories of broken lives, broken hopes, burned bridges, and broken dreams. Some people respond to these with actions that only compound their misfortune, as did those who threw themselves out of a window at the beginning of the Great Depression because their financial aspirations were ruined.

Although not quite in the same vein as someone whose dream depends on a future realization, Fantine in the musical version of *Les Misérables* sings "I dreamed a dream…," yearning and dreaming for something she could never have again, her dream replaced by a life of misery and poverty. She is a dramatic literary example of someone who went from "living the dream" to the nightmare of "this hell I'm living." Yet all is well that ends well and she recovered. At the end of the story she sings "Come with me…" to the man who raised her daughter to adulthood after her premature death. She made it to heaven and was now going to return the favor. The moral of the story is that even if our earthly dreams are shattered, we may still rise like a Phoenix-saint from the ashes of ruin, and there is still another life and another world beyond this earthly reality, a better place in which to hope and where eternal dreams may still come true.

In a television interview on *Firing Line with Margaret Hoover*, supermodel Paulina Porizkova said that "the best things in life aren't easy." The best dreams in life are not easy or cheap. The best dreams in life last into eternity.

Even monks have dreams. I want to learn and grow. I want to become a saint.

> My mission is to become a saint and to extend God's kingdom of love, for the glory of God and the good of all.

It begins with a dream. Then comes prayer.

> Ask and it will be given to you; seek and you will find; knock and the door will be opened to you. For everyone who asks, receives; and the one who seeks, finds; and to the one who knocks, the door will be opened. (Matthew 7:7–8)

Then comes courage and hope.

> Therefore I tell you, all that you ask for in prayer, believe that you will receive it and it shall be yours. (Mark 11:24)

Then comes suffering. Then love.

What is your dream?

2

The Fullness of Time

The Louisiana State University women's basketball team had just won its first-ever national championship, and Kim Mulkey, LSU's second-year head coach, was elated. In an on-court interview after the game, she seemed the personification of joy and gratitude and twice mentioned that she was "blessed."

After a successful tenure as Baylor University women's basketball coach that included three national championships, Mulkey decided it was time to return to her home state of Louisiana when she accepted an offer to become the head coach at LSU. Having won the national championship in only her second year, most agreed she had the program progressing well ahead of schedule.

At a welcome home rally a few days following the NCAA tournament, Mulkey stood on center stage with her team and addressed a crowd that had gathered at the venue where LSU plays its home games. Referring to the fact that she had returned "home" only two years earlier, she said, "Timing is everything in our lives." Mulkey seems to be saying that among her many blessings—and much hard work—she counts good timing as a contributing factor to her success.

Good timing is a blessing that all of us should enjoy, even if very few of us will ever win a national championship. Scripture says that there is a time for everything under the sun:

> A time to give birth, and a time to die;
> a time to plant, and a time to uproot the plant.
> Ecclesiastes 3:2

The ancient Greeks conceived of time as *chronos* and *kairos*. *Chronos* is time kept according to a watch, calendar, or some other instrument of measurement. *Chronos* corresponds to the physical rotations of the Earth on its axis that form our earthly days, and the physical revolutions of the Earth around the sun that give us our earthly years. *Kairos*, on the other hand, is independent of physical movement and quantitative measurement. It is qualitative in character and is illustrated in statements such as "the right time" and "it is high time." *Kairos* time is at work when one is "ready" for a teachable moment. It is at work in the words of Victor Hugo when he wrote: "Nothing is more powerful than an idea whose time has come." And it is at work in God's plan in each of our lives, as it was in Jesus' life when he was born of Mary in the "fullness of time" (Galatians 4:4).

But is it entirely true that "timing is everything," or is it also true, as it is with real estate, that "location is everything"? Perhaps both are true if we understand them in the proper sense, and perhaps neither is true in absolute terms. Perhaps we need both the "right place" and the "right time." Kim Mulkey was certainly in the right place at the right time when she won that national championship.

With respect to Christ's life, while we cannot be entirely sure of the *chronos* of his birth, we know that he was born during the reign of Caesar Augustus, the first and greatest of the Roman emperors and one of Western civilization's most successful leaders. More precisely, we know he was born during the reign of King Herod, who died around 4 BC, which enables us to estimate Christ's birth at 6–4 BC. Likewise, while we cannot be entirely sure of the date of his death, we know he was crucified between 26 and 36 AD when Pontius Pilate was procurator in Judea. Even if we cannot be sure about the *chronos* of Christ's life, we can be sure that he lived entirely in *kairos* time, the "fullness of time," a time prepared for him by God alone.

Jesus, it seems, never had much to worry about when it came to good timing. We can in faith be sure that he was always in the right place at the right time simply because he was always doing God's will. And that is the key: good timing and the right location, or "being in the right place at the right time," are a divine blessing. They are a consequence of doing God's will, or for those who have not yet purposefully aligned themselves to it, a sign of predestination and an opportunity to adjust one's way of life so as to live in accordance with God's plan.

LSU won the final game of that national championship on a Sunday—Palm Sunday—a fact which Coach Mulkey did not fail to mention in her on-court interview immediately following the game. She was in the right place at the right time, and so was Christ on Palm Sunday two thousand years earlier. We should breathe a sigh of relief if we find ourselves in the right place at the right time on our journey of life. If we are not, then we must begin with prayer, for only God can bring us there.

Are you in the right place at the right time in your earthly journey? Is today a Palm Sunday experience for you?

3

The Great Game

It seems to me there is a Great Game being played in society. It is not a game unique to any time or place, nor is it played with material objects as exemplified in the saying: "He or she who dies with the most toys wins." Rather, it is a game that uses immaterial objects such as words, terms, and phrases; reason, logic, and rhetoric; opinions, concepts, and perceptions; lingo, shorthand, buzzwords, and jargon. Since these are a part of everyday life, the Great Game is available for everyone to play. Indeed, you will find it is played at home and abroad, in schools and in the workplace, in academia, government, and politics.

The game is being played out most noticeably in public discourse, especially in the media, and it can also be found in the pages of history. It is not a game that is necessarily enjoyable, although I suspect some people enjoy themselves at it. The Great Game is fundamentally related to the deepest and most profound dynamic in all of human history: the battle between good and evil.

The Great Game is essentially a war of words, rhetoric, and logic. The great field of battle is the hearts and minds of human persons. On one side of the battleground stands truth and all of its accompanying virtues; on the other stands falsity, darkness, ignorance, deceit, and other similar vices. Being largely immaterial yet having material consequences, the Great Game transcends time and place. It is played in the spoken and written word of yesterday, today, and tomorrow.

The stakes of this game are high both in this world and the next. While salvation is the ultimate prize being won and lost, there are important consequences for this world as well. There is much at stake in the culture wars that rage in society today, and the world we fashion will be the one we bequeath to our descendants tomorrow.

None of us can entirely escape participating in the Great Game since all of us are subject to it in one form or another. Edgar Allan Poe among others advised: "Believe nothing you hear, and only half of what you see." I keep this counsel in mind when I read a newspaper or magazine or when I listen to the news on the radio or television. I try to discern what is going on between the lines and in the background. What are the presuppositions to which I am expected to agree? Are my a priori values and perceptions similar to those of the author or commentator? Am I learning anything from this? Will it make me grow? Am I being brainwashed? How does this correspond to my values and what I hold to be good and true? Does this agree with my Christian faith and morals? A healthy dose of intellectual skepticism is a good thing, but not the kind that makes one cynical or jaded.

Almost everything in life is a project and a process, and human life is a continuous process of formation whether we realize it or not. We are constantly being influenced by the stimuli we receive from the world around us, and the way we respond to those stimuli is at least as formative as the stimuli themselves. Everything has the potential to affect me in some way, and it is my responsibility to take control of how my inner life is shaped and influenced. I do not want to lose the Great Game because I was unaware that I was being deceived any more than I want to lose the Great War for the salvation of our souls because I was unaware that I was being misled. I see those two events as intimately connected.

The Descent into Hell

Good terms
Fraternal rapport
Positive regard

MALICE LATENT

Gentle and friendly persuasion

MALICE MANIFEST

Captious and specious reasoning

?

"What exactly
am I dealing
with here?"

Manipulation and deceit

Argument
Assault
Violence

The
Great Game

The way is wide and narrow

Sometimes there is no other solution but punishment

4

The Mystery of Iniquity

Ah, the Great Game…

I have played the Great Game for many years now, studied it like a Grandmaster, perfected it like a Great Champion. I know all of the ins and outs, all of the little tricks of the trade—when to slow down and when to make haste, when to retreat and when to press ahead, when to dissemble and when to be forthright. There is nothing in the Game I have not seen. I know all the moves and when to make them. Timing is everything! Perfecting my craft has for me been a labor of love, so to speak.

There are many of us who play the Great Game. You do not notice us in society very often if at all, and we prefer it that way. We keep our business to ourselves—it makes things run more smoothly. You might think of us as a subcommunity, cave trolls hanging out in dark basements gaming night after night, but you do not realize we enjoy the light of day just as much as you do, and we move in the same circles. Far from being nocturnal and reclusive, we are highly social creatures—industrious and productive, ever concerned for the common good, like a colony of bees helping to build bridges and tear down walls. Always interested in what is best for everyone, we are altruistic in our own way. We hope to change the world as much as others do. Yet for all of our social conformity and responsibility, we remain avidly devoted to the Game.

> Sometimes here and sometimes there
> I am in all places at the same time
> At all times in the same place
> I shroud myself in secrecy by hiding in the open
> The more you notice me, the less you are aware of me
> I am the Artful Dodger
> When it comes to me, you never quite know
> Even if you solve my riddles, I am as evasive as the wind
> Catch me in a bottle and what do you have?

So where is the Great Game played? It is played not in some dark corner of the universe, but in common social discourse and in the light of day. Still, it remains perfectly suited to concealment and dark corners. And therein lies a riddle:

> It is available to all and mastered by none
> For those who master it are mastered by it
> And if one is mastered, one is a slave

The Great Game is played wherever two or three are gathered together and there I am in their midst, even if I am steeped in secrecy. I am the Master of the Game! Learn from me and you will learn from the Greatest. I always know the next move, the next play, the next gambit. My tactics are flawless, as of course is my strategy. My weapons are always righteous, even if I reap where I do not sow and fleece where I do not floss. I am a master of disguise, and my use of language is always in the superlative. Let me show you the secret to my success and I will win you over.

The Great Game is not one of chance
But of skill, intelligence, and daring
One looks deep inside
Where mysteries hide
And brings forth lies for the sharing

I am at once a scientist and a sophist, a warrior and a diplomat, a lion and a sheep, and many other things you cannot bear now. I am sometimes what you want me to be, but never what you think I am. If I cannot have a mile, I will take an inch. If I cannot have an inch, I will take a hair's width. If I cannot turn you 180 degrees, I will turn you one. I do not expect you to be converted to my way of thinking all at once. I am patient. Did I build Rome in a day? A turn of phrase here, a euphemism there, a slight misrepresentation now, an unimportant misinterpretation later, a few minor omissions sprinkled about, and you will see the light. I am equally liberal with red herrings and histrionics as I am with ad hominem and straw man arguments, and I have many other tricks besides. If nothing else, I will dissemble, obfuscate, or temporize, or all three. Darkness is my favorite color. If I mischaracterize, it is only for your good. Misinformation is only harmful when it leads to undesirable results. Learning to see reality in an alternate light will expand your horizons and open new vistas of consciousness, and your cognitive and experiential opportunities will grow endlessly. The slight distortions you notice will dissipate over time and you will grow wise and adaptable under my tutelage. A rose by any other name may not in fact be a rose!

> The Day is done, the game is won
> Come forever to life on the sun
> Yoke them up and bind them tight
> Toss them into the darkness of night

There is much in the world from which I wish to protect you. Do you think I would let you be deceived in the Great Game? Learn from me, for I am sleek and humble of heart! Arrogance will be our national pastime. One witch taught that there are souls the devil tries vigorously, but other souls he leaves in contentment because he knows he has them. Witch! Traitor! How does she know? Let me save you from this blindness and the Great Tyrant and I will make you my true servant!

> Wiggle and waggle
> Bamboozle and dazzle
> Tit for tat and spit for spat
> Grizzle and grime
> Grit and slime
> A penny and dime for a nursery rhyme

Deceit! Thief! Would you allow Them to checkmate you in the Great Game for all eternity? The work of my hands, a cyclops of reason!

I am the mystery of iniquity, a riddle of lies
Learn from me, and you will know nothing
Speak to me, and you will hear nothing
Commune with me, and you will gain nothing
And what will you have but the Father of Lies?

The Sindicate

5

The Junkyard of Broken Dreams

Dear Diary,

Here I find myself in the same place again.

Why is it that every time I begin something new in life, when I set my hopes on something worthwhile, it always ends in failure, disappointment, and sorrow? Nothing in life works out for me, nothing lasts much past an initial stage of hope and enthusiasm. I know that everyone has tough breaks and experiences failure, rejection, and loss at some point in life, but it seems that I am being singled out for a particularly larger portion of these. Why doesn't God bless any of my endeavors?

Oh, there have been times in life when things worked out, more or less, sometimes to my benefit and sometimes to my woe, but nothing of value lasts. I can't seem to build on anything. Any apparent success or accomplishment is fleeting, and all that is left in its wake is loss and dejection. I know there are people in the world who have more difficult lives than I have — some much more — and I know they pick up the pieces and move on, which is what I will do again. I pray for them, and will try to count my blessings.

I have heard it said that God counts effort and not success. Fine! But it would be nice if some of this effort would eventually pay off someday. I have also heard it said that God rewards for labor, hardship, patience, and good will. Great! Is there any possibility that I might receive some reward in this life for all of my effort and trouble?

As I empty myself out on these pages night after night, I sometimes wonder if God hears my prayers. I am beginning to lose willpower. And hope.

Anyway, I will figure out something else to do. I pray for those who experience hardship in life, and I pray for myself.

Are you listening, Lord? Can you hear me?

6

The Train to the Station

I once heard a homily given by a bishop in which he used the children's story, *The Little Engine That Could*, to illustrate his point. The story features a train that repeats the mantra, "I think I can, I think I can" as he pulls another train over a mountain. I do not remember the entire homily because that was so many years ago, but I got the message when he said: "It is not our job to get the train to the station."

As we all know, the point of this story is to teach the value of effort and perseverance, but the bishop's message was that success in the spiritual life and in the service of God depends more on grace and faith than it does on application and effort, and that no one ever became a saint through effort and perseverance alone. What made the homily so memorable for me was that he ardently repeated the statement, "It is not our job to get the train to the station" in a way that paralleled the story's message, "I think I can, I think I can." It seemed that a great weight was lifted from my shoulders that day. I have heard thousands of homilies in my life, but I only remember a handful of them. This is one.

"It's not our job to get the train to the station." It's God's! The Lord said, "Without me you can do nothing" (John 15:5), meaning that success in God's service depends upon his blessing and cooperation. We must nevertheless imitate "the little engine that could" by making a sincere effort, persevering as long as seems reasonable, and most of all having faith in God, in ourselves, and in the good work we are trying to accomplish.

"It's not our job to get the train to the station," but it is our job to lay the track! Success in life may depend upon God, but he is not going to slip into our shoes and do the legwork. Saint Faustina revealed that God rewards for labor, hardship, patience, and good will. He rewards for effort, in this life and the next.

"It's not our job to get the train to the station." I will never forget those words for as long as I live. Just as it is God's job to ensure ultimate success in life, it is by *his* standards that success will be judged. If we want insight into those standards, we have Scripture and the example of those whose lives demonstrated heroic charity.

Abraham Lincoln spoke of "the better angels of our nature." Lincoln was in fact a good example of what the bishop was teaching. He realized that, for all he could do, the final outcome was not his to determine. It was God's job to complete the good work he set out to accomplish in life. It was God's job to get the train to the station.

And it was Lincoln's job to help lay the track.

7

A Primer on the Spiritual Life, Part 1

Modern society has come a long way now that we are able to talk openly about mental health issues without feeling ashamed. Thankfully, the stigma that once surrounded mental health is dissipating and we are able to treat it with the same respect, consideration, and professional concern as we do our physical health. Maybe someday we will be able to express these same sentiments about our spiritual health.

"Spiritual health? . . . Oh, sure, we can just lump that in with mental health."

Well ... yes and no. There is more to the spiritual life than what is found in the study of psychology, and there is more to the psychological sciences than what is treated in the spiritual life. Yet there is overlap, for sure.

The science of the spiritual life is akin to the psychological sciences except that it is conducted in a religious context. The object of study is the same: the incorporeal part of human nature, that is, the psyche, mind, heart, soul, spirit—all of which can be differentiated from one another with some nuance. As a group, however, they are distinguished from the corporeal part of our nature, the human body, which is the object of study of the medical sciences. The spiritual life teaches that the pastor or confessor is the doctor of the soul, which parallels the notion that psychotherapists and other practitioners of the psychological sciences are doctors of the psyche.

Psychology holds that sexuality and aggression are the twin drives of the human personality. Saint Thomas Aquinas discusses concupiscence and irascibility in his *Summa Theologiae* which correspond well, but not precisely, with sexuality and aggression as the twin drives of the human spirit. The origin of all human activity, love, resides deep within the human heart.

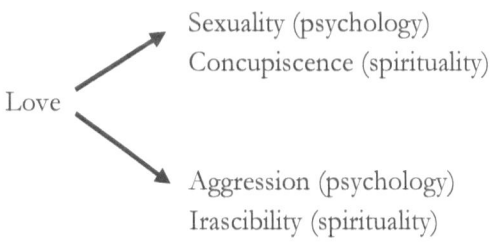

The goal of the psychological sciences can be expressed in different ways: self-realization, self-actualization, mental well-being, and the like. The goal of the spiritual life can also be expressed in various ways: sanctification and purification, personal holiness, perfect charity, union with God, etc. Mental health and spiritual health are closely tied, although one is not the other. It is possible for someone with a high degree of sanctity to experience mental health issues. Likewise, it is possible for someone who is spiritually dead (having lost sanctifying grace) to have no mental health issues of note.

Sanctifying grace is lost through mortal sin and only God can restore it. As the term implies, sanctifying grace brings a person to holiness, which is defined as: (1) a participation in the divine life, and (2) a sharing in the divine nature. Even though God accomplishes all of his acts as Father, Son, and Spirit working together in unison, the work of sanctification is normally attributed to the Holy Spirit. The indwelling of the Holy Spirit must be preserved at all costs, even to the point of physical death. To lose him would result in the spiritual death of the soul.

Spiritual Principle #1: Sanctifying grace is the most precious gift in the spiritual life.

When Christ says in the Gospel, "Without me you can do nothing" (John 15:5), it *seems* counterintuitive to how we operate in our day-to-day lives. It *appears* that we can do a great many things without God, including sin, start wars, ruin the environment, and many other activities he would never help us with. What is more, it *seems* that he is unable to prevent these kinds of things from happening. It is as if he is unable to help himself, that he can do nothing in the world without human agency. Now *seems* and *appears* indicate a matter of perception, and as everyone knows, reality is not always what it *seems* or *appears* to be. Theologically speaking, even though God is omnipotent, he prefers to use human persons to accomplish his will and plan. This is a conundrum, and there are miracles to consider which do not involve human agency, but the point is that God should not be expected to do what humans can do for themselves.

When it comes to sanctifying grace, however, it is we who are unable to help ourselves. "Without me you can do nothing" (John 15:5) means that humans have no power at all to sanctify or consecrate. When it comes to the spiritual life, God reigns supreme and there is truly nothing we can do for ourselves or others without him. We could work our whole lives toward personal holiness and not make one ounce of progress in our prayer life, growth in virtue, personal holiness, or purification on our own. All of this depends upon the work of God.

> **Spiritual Principle #2**: God alone has the power to purify, sanctify, and consecrate.

Yet this does not excuse us from making every effort to become holy. There is no advancement in the spiritual life without discipline and sacrifice. God does not reward for laziness, and there is no such thing as cheap grace. Grace is defined as: (1) God's beneficent help in general, (2) a specific individual gift or favor, and (3) sanctifying grace. It is always gratuitously given, which means God is not obliged to impart it. Additionally, grace never interferes with human freedom or distorts human nature.

> **Spiritual Principle #3**: Grace builds on and perfects nature.

The greatest gift God can give is life itself, which is understood as: (1) temporal life on earth, (2) eternal life in heaven, and (3) holiness or sanctity, which is a participation in God's life and nature. The Christian spiritual tradition holds that perfect charity is the perfection of our lives on earth. Charity, the queen of all the virtues, pertains directly to the two greatest commandments: (1) the love of God, and (2) the love of neighbor and a proper love of self. The Greek word for *love* in the Bible is *agape*, and the Latin word is *caritas*.

Love of God

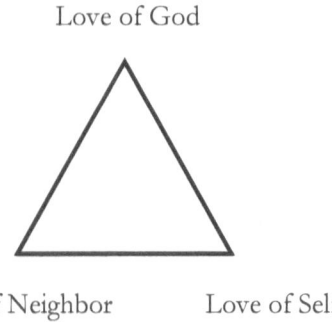

Love of Neighbor   Love of Self

Spiritual Principle #4: Loving humility, or humble love, is the most powerful force in the universe.

Narcissistic self-love is distinguished from an appropriate love of self as vice is distinguished from virtue. Progress in the spiritual life depends upon growth in self-knowledge and learning how to practice a proper love of self, since there is a spiritually healthy way to care for oneself and a selfish way that leads to egoism. Narcissistic self-love is an inversion of the virtue of charity.

Narcissistic, egotistical self-love

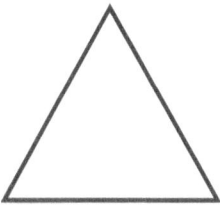

Love of God (if at all)   Love of neighbor (if at all)

Spiritual Principle #5: Narcissistic self-love is the root of all evil.

This spiritual teaching conforms to the discovery in the psychological sciences of the dark triad of psychopathy, narcissism, and Machiavellianism, or if you prefer, the dark tetrad which includes sadism.

8

A Hero Is Chosen

Position(s) available for immediate hire. All applications accepted. The ideal candidates will possess or be able to conform to the following:

- The willingness to do whatever it takes
- Perseverance until the end
- Trust

The following are not required for submission of an application. In many cases, an absence of these may enhance the applicant's desirability:

- Friends
- Close relations
- Popularity
- A regular job
- Any form of income
- A clue
- High social standing
- Distinguishing marks of achievement, advancement, or talent

- A positive reputation
- A highly developed moral life (public notoriety will not serve as grounds for disqualification and in some cases may help to enhance the applicant's desirability provided that he or she is amenable to a program of training and correction)
- Other qualities negotiable

Hiring process and career path as follows:

1. **A Hero Is Chosen.** Employer will choose one or more hero candidates.

2. **Desert Experience.** Candidate will embark upon a desert experience as an apprentice.

3. **Mission and Vocation.** Apprentice will be given a mission and vocation.

4. **Capstone Experience.** Apprentice will be tested.

5. **Deus ex Machina.** Employer will provide assistance as needed.

1. A Hero Is Chosen

"God chose the foolish of the world to shame the wise, and God chose the weak of the world to shame the strong, and God chose the lowly and despised of the world, those who count for nothing, to reduce to nothing those who are something, so that no human being might boast before God." (1 Corinthians 1:27-29)

"He grew up like a sapling before him, like a shoot from the parched earth; He had no majestic bearing to catch our eye, no beauty to draw us to him. He was spurned and avoided by men, a man of suffering, knowing pain, like one from whom you turn your face, spurned, and we held him in no esteem." (Isaiah 53:2-3)

2. Desert Experience

Once hired, apprentice must be willing to accept changes in his or her life and possible relocation. A period of formation is essential for building moral character that will render him or her fit for future responsibilities. Apprentice will begin an extensive program of education, training, and purification. Apprentice may be asked to endure unpleasant living and working conditions that may include long hours; distasteful tasks and assignments; selfish, unreasonable, and immature companions; fasting and abstinence; and other trials and tribulations as required by one's mission and vocation.

Upon completion of desert experience, apprentice may be asked to relocate. Timing and location are everything. Almost. Apprentice is advised that completion of the desert experience does not mean an end to the formation program, as continuing formation in holiness will necessarily last for the remainder of his or her earthly life.

3. Mission and Vocation

Apprentice will embark upon a challenging vocation, and his or her life may change dramatically. Apprentice will complete tasks shared in common with other disciples and may be asked to fulfill at least one unique mission during his or her lifetime. Failure is serious but will not necessarily result in the loss of salvation. Success will be generously rewarded.

The integrity of the apprentice should improve over time. Moral faults should decrease until they are finally extinguished. Errors in judgment should also decrease as apprentice will be expected to grow in intellectual virtue, particularly in reasonableness and right-mindedness, as well as in moral virtue. Failure in intellectual matters is less serious than failure in moral matters, however.

4. Capstone Experience

Apprentice will be required to pass through an event or a series of events that will serve as a capstone experience. Failure is possible in whole or in part, but former apprentices unanimously attest that the experience was well worth the sacrifice.

5. Deus ex Machina

Apprentice will be advised that success in any
endeavor is not entirely up to him or her. It is
not his or her job to get the train to the
station. Apprentice will be reminded that divine
assistance is always available and that he or she
is never alone. Apprentice is advised that divine
providence is more readily poured out during the
most difficult moments in one's life, notably the
capstone experience, hero-event, and hero-moment.

Do you believe in miracles?

Do you want to become a hero-saint?

Then when the chips are down
And the odds are against
When the stakes are high
And the end is near
When everything is on the line
And you are an underdog
Down and out
Alone in the world
Without much going for you
And a long shot to win
When your only options are to overcome or perish
And all you have on your side is God
Then know that you are blessed indeed
The most fortunate being in the universe
Because you are right where God wants you to be
You are in the Hands of God

Never doubt a person of faith
Deus ex machina

9

A Primer on the Spiritual Life, Part 2

Every nature has a perfection, and the perfection of human nature is to be like God. Since we are made in his image and likeness and he is the ultimate good, our goal is to participate in his life and nature as perfectly as possible.

Angels are entirely spiritual beings, meaning they possess no corporeal element (body). Human persons, on the other hand, have a dual nature of both body and soul. With regard to the spiritual life, one of the most important things to know about the body is that the five senses act as windows or channels through which the soul gains knowledge of the outside world. Without the physical senses, the soul would be trapped inside the body as if it were a prisoner in a cell with no windows or doors. An excellent discussion on the five senses and their importance in the spiritual life can be found in the works of Saint John of the Cross.

The soul is the spiritual principle of the body and its principle of life. The word *principle* has two meanings: (1) a fundamental truth, and (2) an origin of activity. To say that the soul is the spiritual principle of the body and its principle of life is to say that the soul is the origin of the body's life and spirit. Without a soul, a body is a corpse.

The soul has three faculties: will, intellect, and memory, the latter being sometimes included with the intellect. Just as the body has five physical senses, there are five spiritual senses in the soul:

1. *The ear is the organ of obedience.* When Scripture says:

> Listen, my people, I will testify against you
> If only you would listen to me, Israel!
>   Psalm 81:9

to listen means *to obey.*

2. *The eyes are the organ of understanding.* When Scripture says:

> They look but do not see and
> hear but do not listen or understand.
>   Matthew 13:13

this means that these people have the spiritual faculty to be capable of understanding but are blinded by sin or obstinacy.

3. *The nose is the organ of intuition.* In common parlance, we say, "I smell a rat," or "Something smells fishy around here." There are many instances in Scripture when God is said to smell a fragrant aroma usually associated with prayer, sacrifice, or holiness (e.g., Genesis 8:21; Exodus 29:18), but it is the human author who intuits whether or not God is pleased.

4. *The mouth is the organ of a direct experience with God and the things of God.* This is evident when Scripture says:

> Taste and see that the Lord is good.
> Psalm 34:9

5. *The sense of touch also refers to a direct experience with God or the things of God.* The Song of Songs is replete with this kind of language, and we also find it when God is said to caress, hold, or carry a human person.

The essence of holiness, according to Saint Faustina, is doing the will of God. This fact could not be overemphasized. To love God is to obey God, and to obey him willingly is to love him, even when one does not feel as if one does. Christ always did the will of his Father and to be Christian or Christ-like is to imitate him in his obedience to God. Obedience to the will of God is the key to living the spiritual life.

> **Spiritual Principle #6**: The essence of holiness is doing the will of God.

Evil is defined in Greek philosophy as the privation of a good that should be there but is absent. It is like a cavity in a tooth, and evil in the spiritual life has the same effect. If the soul is not filled with something spiritually beneficial, it will eventually become infected with vice and finally die. Evil in the spiritual life is the privation of sanctifying grace or virtue that should be there but is not. The reassuring thing about the presence of evil in the world and in our souls is that God would never allow evil to happen unless he intended to draw from it some good.[1] God always has a meaningful response to the mystery of iniquity.

Moral evil exists in the world because human beings have free will and God does not take it away from us. Free will gives us the capacity to cooperate with God or defeat his plan for our lives. If human beings did not have free will, we would be no better than robots or slaves, and that is not what God wants. He seeks willing participants in his plan for creation and salvation, not captives or hostages. While grace builds on and perfects nature, it never obliterates it. God will never take away or destroy what he has created, including our free will, which is precisely what the spiritual forces of darkness are trying to do.

> **Spiritual Principle #7**: The deepest and most fundamental principle in all of history is the perpetual opposition between good and evil.

The literature of the Christian tradition teaches at length on the constant warfare between good and evil that has always existed in the world. This self-evident truth manifests itself in the life of every human person in the form of spiritual combat that is impossible for anyone to escape. The study of history and current events shows how much warfare and sin of all kinds there has been among humans in all ages, all of which occur because there is a battle occurring within each of us between good and evil. Anyone devoted to living the spiritual life knows that spiritual

---

[1] *Catechism of the Catholic Church*, #324.

combat is ever-present. These phenomena are related. The impetus for our external actions comes from within.

The enemies of the soul are the devil, the flesh, and the world. The devil and other fallen angels are real and it is dangerous to believe otherwise. Humanity is prepared to spend trillions of dollars on space exploration ostensibly to discover if there are other lifeforms in the universe. How can we on one hand investigate the possibility of extraterrestrial life at such great effort and expense, yet on the other hand refuse to believe in the existence of spiritual beings here on earth? Have we become so utterly materialistic? If you learn nothing else from this book, please at least accept that fallen angels exist and they are our enemies. What we do not know can in fact hurt us.

Spiritual Principle #8: The enemies of the soul are the devil, the flesh, and the world.

The devil is portrayed in Scripture as a liar and a murderer. All of his deeds originate from his malice which is beyond anything we can experience in human-to-human interaction. His hatred and ill will are of another order entirely and are terrifying to the point of paralysis. This is because the devil is far more powerful than any human being, and it only stands to reason that his power to hate and propensity for violence is far greater than any human being could ever possess.

Scripture is clear in its teaching that the devil deceives and kills. As a murderer, he seeks to destroy sanctifying grace in the soul, thus creating a cavity—a privation of a good that should be there but is absent—which will eventually corrupt the soul. As a liar, he and his henchmen seek to distort reality, little by little, gradually, by small steps, over time. The work of destruction can be the work of a lifetime. You will find the spiritual forces of darkness operative in misinformation, misrepresentation, misinterpretation, mischaracterization, and other such subtleties as much as you will find them in visibly violent actions. The devil hates the light, and there are times when mere opinion is the enemy of God and truth. The common advice: "Believe nothing you hear, and only half of what you see" and "Do not believe everything you think" are worth considering.

The devil and other evil spirits have access to the imagination and the sensibilities when they tempt, but they can only solicit the will, neither controlling it nor determining it. The will exists at all times in a state of relative freedom depending on how ingrained the habit of virtue or vice is in the soul. The more virtuous a soul is, the greater the person's freedom (i.e., the power to choose the good). The more vicious a soul is, the more the person is a slave to the power of sin and the devil's influence. In cases of possession where the devil has greater power over the soul, the will remains somewhat free even if that freedom is minimized and the soul is weak. God will not allow the devil to actually control a person's free will. Movies are not a good source of information on this topic.

The second enemy of the soul is the flesh which is defined as: (1) anything opposed to grace, and (2) the skin and soft tissue of the human body as distinguished from bone. When Saint Paul says that "the flesh has desires against the Spirit, and the Spirit against the flesh; these are opposed to each other, so that you may not do what you want" (Galatians 5:17), he means the flesh is everything in us opposed to grace. When he writes about his "thorn in the flesh" (2 Corinthians 12:7), he is probably referring to some kind of physical ailment, perhaps from having endured so much physical hardship, or maybe a congenital condition or injury. We simply do not know.

The third enemy of the soul, the world, is understood in two senses in the Christian tradition, a neutral one and a pejorative one. The world in a neutral sense is comprised of people, places, things, ideas, events, and occurrences. This sense is used when Scripture says: "For God so loved the world that he gave his only Son, so that everyone who believes in him might not perish but might have eternal life" (John 3:16). In the pejorative sense, the world is all that is opposed to God's kingdom in human societies of all ages.

Associated with the world are worldly goods which are acquired for their own ends and inflame the pride and sensuality of the possessor. These include riches, honors, pleasures, power, status, and fame. In contrast to temporal, worldly goods are spiritual goods and their beneficial effects which are meant to endure into eternity. These include graces, virtues, merits, glory, honor, and indulgences. Spiritual goods are not to be confused, however, with the goal of the spiritual life, nor are they more important than sanctifying grace. The goal is always personal holiness, sanctification and purification, perfect charity, spiritual perfection, or perfect union with God's will. Spiritual goods are meant to help us toward our ultimate goal and to reward us for serving God.

Obedience to God's will and authentic discipleship also bring meaning, value, purpose, fulfillment, reward, and satisfaction in life. These should be considered as spiritual benefits in addition to the spiritual goods.

10

Mindfulness and the Practice of the Presence of God

The practice of mindfulness has become popular today as a means of psychotherapeutic treatment and as a form of meditation for those who are simply looking to enhance their lives. Mindfulness is religiously neutral in the sense that it does not explicitly teach or advocate religious principles, but it is certainly compatible with religion and spiritual discipline. It has probably been known for centuries by monks and yogis of every stripe, and it may go back to the origins of our species when human beings first developed the capacity for self-consciousness.

Nicolas Herman was born in 1614 in France. His early life was marked by poverty and violence not unusual for medieval and early-modern Europe. He grew into manhood during the Thirty Years War (1618–1648), a complicated and highly destructive conflict fought mostly in central Europe. In order to feed himself, Herman was forced into soldiery. Wounded and almost killed, he experienced a religious awakening that eventually led him in 1640 to join the Discalced Carmelite Priory in Paris. Having no education, he became a lay brother and took the name Brother

Lawrence of the Resurrection. His life was one of manual work, simple prayer, and service to his religious community. He is known to us today as the author of the Christian classic, *The Practice of the Presence of God*, which was compiled from his letters and conversations. He passed away in 1691.

The title of this book captures the main idea. Brother Lawrence's spiritual discipline is a meditative technique one might summarize as mindfulness practiced in a religious way that stresses the habit of purposely turning one's mind to God so as to be continually aware of his presence. As soon as he became aware that his mind had wandered, he refocused his attention back on God's presence. Like mindfulness, this practice is as simple as it is profound and life-changing. Like mindfulness, it is as difficult to do as it is simple.

Many years ago I heard an interview on the radio with a Buddhist monk who said his main spiritual discipline was the continuous practice of patience. This is worth mentioning here because of its compatibility with mindfulness and the practice of the presence of God. Buddha did not claim to be a god, but he did profess to be awake. Mindfulness stresses wakefulness, and Brother Lawrence tried to be continuously awake to the presence of God. What seems apparent is that mindfulness, practicing the presence of God, and practicing continual patience share common ground, namely wakefulness, awareness of the present moment, patience, self-control, and mental relaxation.

Mindfulness can be both a treatment and a way of life. Psychotherapeutic treatment utilizes the practice of mindfulness to improve mental and physical health. For patients, the goal of mindfulness is the alleviation of ailments such as anxiety, depression, posttraumatic stress disorder, chronic physical pain, and substance addictions, but the goal of mindfulness, germane to everyone, is to live more fully in the present moment, to be more aware of ourselves and our surroundings, and to gain a higher level of consciousness. Practitioners of mindfulness also advocate:

- A wholesome curiosity and openness to the world around us

- Becoming aware of psychic sensations and physical discomfort and viewing it all with a non-judgmental attitude

- The observation of thoughts and a dissociation of those thoughts with the true self.

~

All of this to say that if your dream is to become a Jedi Monk, then you must practice mindfulness, the presence of God, and most of all patience.

Jedi Knights and Jedi Monks have much in common:

- Jedi Knights serve and are guided by the Force, which has a light and dark side. Jedi Monks serve and are guided by God, who is only Light.

- The self-discipline and training of Jedi Knights compares with the spiritual and corporal discipline maintained by Jedi Monks, except that Jedi Monks do not kill anyone, not even droids.

- In trying to get in touch with the Force, Jedi Knights engage in a form of mindfulness and meditation that is akin to prayer and listening with the ear of the heart. Jedi Monks try to connect with God through meditative prayer and contemplation and have a rich tradition upon which to draw.

- Jedi Knights are taught Christian virtues such as patience, compassion, humility, modesty, prudence, altruism, charity, temperance, chastity, and courage, to name a few. A true Jedi Monk embodies all of these and, like Jedi Knights, practices what Taoism calls effortless doing.

- A true Jedi Monk is a match for the true Jedi Knight in virtue, self-discipline, and in every other respect except that Jedi Monks do not wield lightsabers.

And most of all, each practices patience, trusting in the slow process of sanctification or becoming one with the Force, and trusting in the work of time.

May the Spirit be with you!

11

Perseverance and Self-Will

There is a world of difference between faith and perseverance rooted in good will on one hand, and stubbornness and obstinacy rooted in self-will on the other. The difference at times can be extreme and at other times subtle. There are moments when good will and self-will are short-lived, and instances when one attitude prevails over the course of a lifetime. In any case, the consequences of decisions taken in one disposition or the other can be profound.

In this reflection, I offer two historical examples of famous and influential men—Saint Paul and Mohandas Gandhi—whose lives demonstrate that decisions taken with an attitude of good will or self-will can have far-reaching consequences, even affecting the lives of millions of people and history itself. From the perspective of the spiritual life, we may study their opinions and decisions and the resulting outcomes to attempt to recognize how intimate the connection is between self-will and living in the flesh on one hand, and good will and living in the spirit on the other (Romans 8:5).

In 1940, Gandhi said: "The word *defeat* is not in my vocabulary." Yet a little study of his life using reputable sources shows that he experienced many defeats, both great and small. The taste of defeat and disappointment must have been in his mouth in 1912 when he said: "How despicable my countrymen are." His experience of struggle and failure and the discord between India's politicians of his day must have prompted him to say in 1929: "Pray to God to relieve us from the curse of disunity."

His worst defeats were yet to come, however. During the partition of India, which he opposed, and the creation of the new nation of Pakistan, Hindus and Muslims migrated in and out of the territory that is now Pakistan resulting in extensive ethnic and religious violence. Gandhi worked toward the mitigation of the violence, yet many of both faiths lost their homes and livelihoods, and even their lives, despite his best efforts.

If Gandhi knew much about defeat, he also knew something about personal failure. In 1940, he said: "Is there any man who does not bungle?" The movement of India toward independence from Britain was difficult to navigate and Gandhi did not have the benefit of hindsight, but many historians today believe that his unrealistic goals (e.g., his desire to return India to a pre-industrial age and his insistence that a majority of India's citizen live a simple life of manual labor)—well-meaning though he may have been— contributed to the suffering and turmoil of the times. Gandhi clung steadfastly to idealistic but impractical policies and was unwilling to compromise during the political debates before the partition. Had he made a few concessions, the partition and the ensuing violence and loss of life and property might have been averted. In a BBC documentary about Gandhi, a male citizen of India admitted what is perhaps a typical view of many of India's citizens: "Gandhi's ideas do not work."

Yet if there are instances of intransigence in Gandhi's life, there is also a legacy of patient endurance and committed action in the face of injustice, and it is for this that he will be forever remembered. His practice of Satyagraha—passive resistance and devotion to the truth—challenged the rule of British civil authorities and helped pave the way for the independence of India. It is ironic that Gandhi was influenced by the American transcendentalist Henry David Thoreau in developing his understanding of Satyagraha. Thoreau wrote *Civil Disobedience*, a short essay first published in 1849, twenty years before Gandhi's birth. Had he been alive, Thoreau would have looked on Gandhi's non-violent demonstrations with great satisfaction.

In asserting that he would not admit the word *defeat* into his vocabulary, Gandhi is indicating his willingness to persevere despite setbacks and hardships. He shared this quality with his contemporary and political adversary, the indomitable Winston Churchill, himself a model of perseverance and inflexibility, who spoke these words in 1941:

> [T]his is the lesson: never give in, never give in... Never give in except to convictions of honor and good sense... We have only to persevere to conquer.

~

In the New Testament writings, we see evidence of the stubborn self-will of an orthodox Jew named Saul that eventually gave way to the patient endurance of a Christian named Paul and his willingness to endure hardship for Christ's sake. By his own admission, Saul vigorously persecuted the incipient Christian Church prior to his conversion on the way to Damascus. After consenting to the murder of Stephen, he went to the high priest in Jerusalem and "asked him for letters to the synagogues in Damascus, that, if he should find any men or women who belonged to the Way, he might bring them back to Jerusalem in chains" (Acts 9:2). It was on this journey that Paul experienced his famous conversion.

The drastic change from persecuting Pharisee to Christian missionary launched Paul on a course of conflict, controversy, and eventually a violent death. His first battles were fought in Damascus to gain the acceptance and confidence of fellow Jewish Christians.

> All who heard him were astounded and said, "Is not this the man who in Jerusalem ravaged those who call upon this name, and came here expressly to take them back in chains to the chief priests?" (Acts 9:21)

Paul's public witness to Jesus as the Messiah only alienated him from former friends and associates. The "Jews"—those who did not accept Jesus as the Messiah and remained faithful to the traditional Mosaic Law—objected fiercely to his conversion which they naturally viewed as a betrayal of orthodox Judaism. Paul's apparent apostasy earned him such strong censure that "the Jews conspired to kill him, but their plot became known to Saul" (Acts 9:23–24). With the help of other Christian Jews, Paul was able to escape over the walls of Damascus and return to Jerusalem.

The enemies Paul made within orthodox Judaism, not only in Damascus but throughout the Diaspora, were for life. Once in Jerusalem, he again had difficulty earning the trust of fellow Christian Jews, and again faced hostility from traditional Jews who would not accept his conversion. A fresh set of controversies arose from a faction within the early Christian Church called the Judaizers who insisted on the circumcision of adult male converts and strict adherence to the Mosaic Law.

I began this reflection by asserting that there is a world of difference between faith and perseverance rooted in good will on one hand, and stubbornness rooted in self-will on the other. In Scripture we find the same idea in John 3:6: "What is born of flesh is flesh and what is born of spirit is spirit." Faithful perseverance is of the spirit, while obstinacy is of the flesh, which is all that is opposed to grace. The former is rooted in benevolence, the latter something more akin to ill will. The spirit was operative in Paul, the flesh in Saul.

The man Saul was a murderer whose heart was filled with religious pride. In his arrogance, he justified the murder of Stephen and the mistreatment of others whose only offense was

to accept Jesus as the Messiah. His observance of the Torah and
its hundreds of precepts justified in his mind the violation of one
of the ten great commandments of the Mosaic Law: "You shall
not kill" (Exodus 20:13). In his blind self-will and intractability, he
was incapable of true charity, just as his "breathing murderous
threats" (Acts 9:1) is entirely contradictory to the two greatest
commandments.

The man Paul, on the other hand, demonstrated a virtuous
kind of long-suffering and patient endurance that eradicates self-
serving egoism. Paul displayed a sacrificial spirit in his service to
God that could only have been rooted in a divinely inspired
mission and vocation. In his own words:

> Five times at the hands of the Jews I received forty lashes
> minus one. Three times I was beaten with rods, once I
> was stoned, three times I was shipwrecked, I passed a
> night and a day on the deep; on frequent journeys, in
> dangers from rivers, dangers from robbers, dangers from
> my own race, dangers from Gentiles, dangers in the city,
> dangers in the wilderness, dangers at sea, dangers among
> false brothers; in toil and hardship, through many
> sleepless nights, through hunger and thirst, through
> frequent fasting, through cold and exposure. And apart
> from these things, there is the daily pressure upon me of
> my anxiety for all the churches. Who is weak, and I am
> not weak? Who is led to sin, and I am not indignant?
> (2 Corinthians 11:24–29)

Living in the spirit is a source of life and grace while living in
the flesh brings ruin. There can be a fine line between holy

perseverance and inflexibility rooted in self-will which Paul seemingly was able to distinguish when he wrote: "Love ... does not seek its own interests" (1 Corinthians 13:5). Self-will is always self-interested in some way and demonstrates a lack of humility, while faithful perseverance in the spirit is altruistic and centered on God. Paul's conversion brought life and grace to himself and others. As he was approaching the end of his mission he was able to rejoice: "I have competed well; I have finished the race; I have kept the faith" (2 Timothy 4:7).

12

Christianity in Decline

A brief review of the literature regarding the state of Christianity in the Western world today is not encouraging. Research indicates that the number of Christian churches in the United States and Europe is declining along with the number of adults who attend Sunday religious services. Research conducted on the younger generation is even more disheartening. While the data cannot tell us conclusively what the Christian Church will look like in the future, it does point in a problematic direction.

It appears that Christianity is at a crossroads. In a world where societies around the globe are becoming increasingly more interconnected, Christianity seems to be suffering from a problem of disconnect that results in congregants leaving the pews. As science, technology, and scholarship are constantly expanding the limits of human knowledge, the Christian Church has struggled to keep its knowledge relevant in an ever-evolving world. Part of the challenge Christianity faces in the twenty-first century is that its knowledge is fundamentally different from knowledge valued by secular society. In addition, Christian culture is largely determined by its historical roots, while modern culture is moving toward a future that is progressively less dependent on its historical roots.

Christianity's founding documents are Scripture and the writings of early Christian missionaries and theologians. Whenever the Church reflects on its sacred writings and tradition, it begins by looking back thousands of years to ancient Israel and the formation of the Hebrew Scriptures, or what we know as the Old Testament. From there, Christian history progresses through the apostolic age and the formation of the New Testament, into late antiquity, the Middle Ages, and finally into modern times. Church documents have been compiled throughout this long history, and once doctrine has been firmly established, Church authority has historically been resistant to the alteration of accepted orthodox content. This is necessary when it comes to divine revelation because the Holy Spirit reveals truths that cannot be changed. Like the other major world religions, Christianity is founded in its history and adheres firmly to its sacred documents.

The world's documents, on the other hand, whether they concern science, government, or any other branch of knowledge, are subject to modification, revocation, and relegation to the dustbin of history. Theories, social systems, constitutions, treatises, and the like come and go. New documents are created and old ones amended or abolished. Once-revolutionary books become outdated and lay unused on dusty library shelves. Life moves on and so does the world.

This dynamic between Christianity's largely permanent and metaphysical knowledge and the secular world's mutable and chiefly material knowledge fosters a troubling disconnect that intensifies a cultural dissonance. The Church tends to be historically minded, reflecting upon and preserving its tradition and looking to the past for its knowledge. It has demonstrated a historical tendency to resist change, sometimes forcefully, and has not readily accepted the explosion of knowledge that began with the scientific and industrial revolutions. The world, conversely, is inclined to be forward-thinking. It seeks new discoveries and technologies that will hopefully lead to the improvement of earthly life. Toward this end, it embraces scientific, industrial, economic, and social progress and strives relentlessly toward future possibilities.

Not only is the world's knowledge increasing, but its rate of growth is increasing, exacerbating the ever-widening disconnect between religious knowledge and secular knowledge. Who knows what quantum computing, artificial intelligence, robotics, drones, and space exploration will someday bring to the world, but it will not be favorable to the Church. As secular knowledge is growing exponentially and becoming more interesting, attractive, and lucrative, religious knowledge is fundamentally static since it leaves little room for innovation. Even if there is some room for the development of doctrine, there are many teachings that can never be altered without changing the nature of Christianity itself.

Christianity, for better or worse, is firmly rooted in its history and at times is dominated by it. While some members of the Church, notably its authority, have extensive knowledge of Christian history and tradition, the majority of people in society do not read or study history, much less Church history, and know very little about it. Most Christians know even less about Israel's historical roots and how the Old Testament developed, nor do they know much about the history of the Mediterranean world during the first century AD when the New Testament was being written. Although Christianity is steeped in history, most Christians cannot place the Bible in its historical context.

This unfortunate disconnect in knowledge, history, and culture between the Church and the world exists within the Church itself. If one were to read widely in popular Church history and then turn to books written by professional historians, he or she would find a different world. Similarly, those who read hagiographical literature may be inspired to grow closer to God in their spiritual life, but they may also know very little about the history of Western civilization, just as those who read Arthurian legend may understand very little of the actual medieval world.

When the Church is not looking back to an earlier era, it gives more consideration to eternal life than it does to the temporal world of tomorrow. The world, on the other hand, focuses on contemporary events and future earthly life, and even human life on Mars, far more than it considers antiquity and life after death. Secular culture has historical roots, but it is striving to break free from those roots and launch itself into the seemingly endless horizons of tomorrow's possibilities.

Knowledge, history, and culture are key areas of disconnect between Christianity and the world, but which will prevail? Will Christian culture and doctrine somehow reverse the current trend and finally triumph over its modern secular rival, or will today's ever-evolving societies persist in pushing Christianity off to the side, perhaps someday making it archaic, as the world continues its relentless march of progress virtually unimpeded toward a future of its own making? Or perhaps there will be a medium, happy or not, where Christianity survives as a smaller Church but not necessarily a purer one.

Yet being at a crossroads is nothing new for Christianity. It has been here many times over the past two thousand years and has always survived. While there is cause for pessimism, there is still reason to hope.

Charles Darwin once wrote: "It is not the strongest species that survive, nor the most intelligent, but the ones most responsive to change." If the Christian Church is going to survive into the twenty-second century, then resilience and adaptability will be as necessary as strength and intelligence. The fundamental problem of the Church in the modern world is that it is usually behind the times and gets pulled along by the movement of contemporary events into a future it has a habit of resisting and rejecting. But time is of the essence now, and the future is not so far away. If Christianity is to flourish, it must adapt and be responsive to change. I am not advocating a change in doctrine, but changes in preaching and public worship should be considered.

13

Five Suggestions

Problems are not defeats, and challenges are not failures. No success in any endeavor, great or small, was achieved without solving problems and overcoming obstacles. We all do this every day of our lives. Failure only occurs when we are unable to solve our problems, and defeat only when we are overcome by our challenges.

The problems Christianity faces today are not insoluble, nor are the obstacles insurmountable. What appears to be a weakness can sometimes be turned into a strength, or at least an opportunity for growth. The challenge in the twenty-first century will be to keep the Christian message relevant in an evolving world, and with some creativity, right-mindedness, and willingness to adapt, Christianity may still thrive.

I offer here five suggestions that will improve preaching and public worship and help to stem, if not reverse, the decline in church attendance:

1. *Public worship should be a time of prayer and not performance.*

The world has many events, shows, and other forms of entertainment with which the Church cannot and should not compete, but the Church offers public and private prayer and an experience with God that leads to salvation, and that is something the world generally does not offer.

Festive and triumphant Church celebrations that sometimes become loud are not prayerful, however, nor do they compete well with the celebrations and festivities of the world. The minister should not play the role of a performer, but the leader of common prayer, and the music should be prayerful and not performance-oriented. God should always remain the center of attention in public prayer just as he is in private prayer, and the temptation to eclipse him as the center of attention should be resisted. The Christian Church can learn much from the monastic way of communal prayer.

2. *The key to successful evangelization is better preaching.*

When people come to church, they seek a direct experience with God, a numinous experience, something otherworldly that makes the practice of organized religion meaningful. Preaching that is designed to evoke a warm, emotional response but does not provide intellectual stimulation often becomes uninspiring and even insipid. Constructive preaching is more than giving another bland talk on some basic idea in the Christian life. People want creativity, originality, and fresh intellectual content. Likewise, preaching theological jargon and juggling biblical metaphors, symbols, and imagery can never substitute for knowledge acquired from the study of reliable historical and biblical scholarship. A Church of signs and symbols cannot expect to retain its membership in the modern world of concrete ideas. We must be a Church of authentic learning that contemporary people find invigorating.

The key to better preaching is to incorporate sources outside of theology, Scripture study, and Christian spirituality. The same style and formulations, true and wholesome though they are, will produce the same results. Albert Einstein is commonly credited with having said that insanity is doing the same thing over and over again and expecting different results. If we hope to have a new evangelization, then we will have to try something new. Perhaps Pope Francis had this sentiment in mind when he wrote:

> The homily is the touchstone for judging a pastor's closeness and ability to communicate to his people. We know that the faithful attach great importance to it, and that they and their ordained ministers suffer because of homilies: the laity from having to listen to them and the clergy from having to preach them! It is sad that this is the case. The homily can actually be an intense and happy experience of the Spirit, a consoling encounter with God's Word, a constant source of renewal and growth.

3. *Public address does not have to be long to be effective.*

Franklin Delano Roosevelt's advice to his son regarding public speaking was: "Be sincere, be brief, be seated." Lincoln's Gettysburg Address consists of only 272 words and took two minutes to deliver, yet it is remembered as one of the greatest speeches in American history. Edward Everett, who preceded Lincoln and spoke for two hours, said to Lincoln afterward: "I wish that I could flatter myself that I had come as near to the central idea of the occasion, in two hours, as you did in two minutes." Both of these presidents are recognized as two of the greatest public speakers in American history, and their counsel and example on the brevity of public speaking is as worthwhile today as it was when they were in office. Perhaps they understood that:

> Where words are many, sin is not wanting;
> but those who restrain their lips do well.
> Proverbs 10:19

4. *Those who preach should read.*

Preachers would be performing an act of charity toward themselves and their congregations if they read for an hour a day and kept a notebook of important insights and anecdotes that can be woven into their homilies and sermons. Congregations would benefit from their pastors' reading. Preaching theology, Scripture, and Christian spirituality is necessary, but insights into the human condition can be gleaned from other disciplines as well. Books written by professional historians, particularly those from Oxford and Cambridge and British authors in general, are most rewarding. Students of history are not backward-looking to a fault, but forward-thinking, and tend to agree with the saying: "History does not repeat itself, but it rhymes." There are other subjects worth reading, including current events, and psychology can be especially useful, although these books should be chosen with caution.

By making this suggestion, I do not intend that sermons and homilies should be about history, psychology, current events, or any other subject. I only suggest that homilies and sermons on Christian topics should be informed and enriched by the pastor's learning in other disciplines, and that dedication to a reading schedule would on the whole improve the quality of preaching in the Church substantially. Who would not agree with Saint Ambrose, a Father of the Church, when he teaches: "He who reads much and understands much, receives his full. He who is full, refreshes others."[2]

Yet reading takes time, and for some, it will involve a change in life. This is the hard part. It is here that we must invoke the sacrificial spirit of Christianity. To read for an hour a day while taking notes is asking much from pastors whose schedules are

---

[2] "Memorial of Saint Ambrose," Office of Readings, December 7, *The Liturgy of the Hours,* vol. 1, (New York: Catholic Book Publishing Company, 1975), 1219.

packed with obligations and events. Ministry is time-consuming, and the trend of decreasing vocations intensifies the problem. The burden of sacrifice should not rest on ministers alone, but the faithful must also make concessions. Laity should be advised to make only reasonable requests of their pastors and ministers. Many social "obligations" could and should be dispensed with in favor of reading and pastoral development, and there is some "ministry" that is redundant and unnecessary. If Churches made an effort to explain this to their congregations, the vast majority of church-goers would comply and make only reasonable requests of their pastors with the hope that preaching would improve.

5. *The intellectual content must be elevated.*

An elderly woman once advised a newly ordained minister to "bring those cookies down a few shelves." If she meant to dumb down his homilies, then this was not good advice. Elderly people who have faithfully attended liturgies and services throughout their lives should be well-versed in Christian teaching. It should not be necessary to dumb it down. The philosopher and university lecturer Immanuel Kant provided a good example to teachers by orienting his lectures to the intellectual level of the middle of the class where most of the students are. The brightest students, he surmised, will understand whatever you teach, and the least gifted students will not understand no matter how simple you make it. There is wisdom here for preachers.

Preaching on Sundays should be aimed at the people who make the decisions in the household and drive themselves and others to church. Sunday preaching should be directed toward the average intellectual capacity of the adults in the congregation. These are the parishioners we must win over and keep. Dumbing down homilies and sermons, unless it is a children's liturgy or service, will not reverse the trend of declining church enrollment. The children of the congregation will attend with their parents whether they understand or not, and they will eventually grow intellectually anyway.

Long gone are the days when the priest or minister was the most educated person in his town or village. It was not so long ago when literacy was restricted to fortunate individuals with some wealth and leisure time. Today, literacy is universal and ministers are fortunate if they are among the most knowledgeable people in their parish. The egalitarian nature of knowledge in the twenty-first century would have been unthinkable to previous generations.

Homilies and sermons must be tailored to the congregation to which they are delivered, and people in the modern world are intelligent and knowledgeable. It takes time and hard work to write a good public address. Winston Churchill once admitted that he spent eighteen hours preparing for a forty-five-minute speech in Parliament. That computes to twenty-four hours of preparation for every hour of public speaking. Perhaps this is out of reach for most ministers, but Churchill was a busy man too!

~

I have offered five meaningful suggestions in this reflection that, if adopted by Church leaders and promulgated within their congregations, would be welcomed and embraced by a majority of parishioners and have beneficial and far-reaching effects. Evangelists must become better at delivering the Christian message to an evolving congregation or church attendance in the Western world will continue to decline. This will require adaptation and new techniques.

It takes a strong person to be adaptable and resilient, and as Churchill once said: "The battle in the end must be to the strong."

14

A Primer on the Spiritual Life, Part 3

We have all been to the "school of hard knocks" at one time or another. Some of us took care to study its lessons, some of us moved on before we absorbed them. Many of those lessons can only be taught in the school of hard knocks and nowhere else. Wisdom, or living according to the realities of existence, is a matter of both knowledge and experience, and not all experience can be gained in a formal classroom setting. The school of hard knocks is a place of learning and growth. Where would we be without it?

Benedictine monks have another school of learning and growth which Saint Benedict calls "the school of the Lord's service." This school also involves hard knocks. Those who walk the path of true discipleship attend both schools, and it is here that they receive a formation in integrity and holiness.

True discipleship, or the practice of religion, involves the two main categories of faith and morals. The word *faith* has three meanings: (1) a gift infused by God directly into our soul at baptism along with hope and charity; (2) a virtue, and like all other virtues, it is strengthened when practiced and atrophies when it is neglected; and (3) doctrinal teaching, or religion in general, as exemplified in "the Christian faith" or to "practice one's faith."

Some people do not have faith or lose it because they think they do not have the intellectual grounds for believing in God. They should know that there are three things whose existence cannot be proved using human reason alone: God, the human soul, and life after death. Theologians have devised "convincing and converging arguments"[3] that support the existence of all three, but sometimes the only way to believe in God is to get down on one's knees and pray. Faith in God is more a matter of living a life of faith, turning to God and treating him as if he exists, than it is trying to arrive at intellectual proofs for his existence.

One may have noticed from this brief primer on the spiritual life that it has something of a dualistic nature. Psalm 1 speaks of two paths in life: the way of the righteous and the way of the wicked. If this dualistic tendency of the spiritual life makes it sound simplistic, think again. Remember that at their very foundation, computers operate on a binary system (1/0) and there is a universe of complexity that follows from this dualism. Likewise, the spiritual life may sound simple, but it is very complex, and human life is anything but simple or simplistic.

---

[3] *Catechism of the Catholic Church*, #31.

Einstein is commonly believed to have said that the definition of genius is taking the complex and making it simple, and that if you cannot explain something in simple terms, you do not really understand it. Knowledge does not have to be abstruse to be profound. I will have more to say about the dualistic nature of the spiritual life later.

In truth, knowledge of the spiritual life is the most important knowledge one can possess. It does not pay the bills for most people, but it will help us to gain salvation, and is there anything more important in life than securing eternal salvation?

The science of the spiritual life is the science of salvation. In our short-sightedness, we often see only what is important to us in our earthly lives, and while earthly realities have temporal importance, eternal and spiritual realities should rank higher on our priority list. It is easy for us to lose sight of seemingly remote considerations when there are so many exigencies that require our immediate attention, yet if we spend years preparing for retirement, should we not also prepare for eternity that will last infinitely longer?

We should at all times have a clear understanding of our priorities in life because priorities have a determining effect on our behavior. Relationships should be our highest priority, above all our relationship with God. Psychologists tell us that connecting with others leads to happiness, and so it seems that the need to connect is part of human nature, but it is also a part of our nature to be religious beings, which means that we need to connect with

God even more than with other humans. Connecting with God, in truth, leads to the greatest possible happiness as well as to eternal salvation. We may not experience that happiness in the short term, and the cross is always a part of authentic discipleship, but if our priorities are aligned correctly, we should be willing to delay gratification in the service of God and for the sake of our eternal welfare and those who God calls us to serve.

> **Spiritual Principle #9**: Relationships are the most important priority in life, especially our relationship with God.

A number of the saints have taught that there is nothing small in the spiritual life. There is much, on the other hand, that is unimportant and even trivial in our earthly lives and will not matter at judgment. Little things mean a great deal in the spiritual life. Little acts of charity, forgiveness, self-denial, kindness. Little victories over evil add up because acts form habits, and habits form dispositions, and dispositions form character, and according to the Greek philosopher Heraclitus, character is destiny. Free will has a self-determining characteristic to it. We shape the kind of person we become and participate in our own formation.

> **Spiritual Principle #10**: There is nothing small in the spiritual life.

> **Spiritual Principle #11**: Acts form habits, habits form dispositions, dispositions form character, and character is destiny.

The beginning is the most important. By this I mean that if we get off to a good start, half the battle is won, but if we procrastinate or cut corners in the beginning, we will always be working from behind the eight ball.

Saint Bernard was in the habit of telling himself regularly that now was the moment when he would begin to live the spiritual life, and Saint John Vianney said upon rising every morning that he had to start all over again in the spiritual life. Every journey begins with the first step, and the journey to God's kingdom always begins today, always in the present moment. Jean Pierre de Caussade taught that every present moment is a sacrament of the presence of God.

15

Friendship with God

In Genesis, God tells us that it is not good for a human person to be alone (2:18). He said this to Adam in the Garden of Eden before he created Eve to be his companion. The strict interpretation of this passage refers to marriage between man and woman, but there is a more general interpretation that also applies —that it is not good for a person to be without companionship of one kind or another.

Human beings are communal in nature, social and relational creatures, and we know that no person is an island. This being so, I interpret Genesis 2:18 to mean that all human beings should have at least one person in whom they can confide. This interpretation corresponds with James 5:16 which advises members of the early Church to "confess your sins to one another," not because it is helpful for the community to know the sins of others, but because it is beneficial for those confessing. Those who have ever sought counseling know that merely telling one's problems to another person has in itself a healing property even if there is nothing the counselor can say or do to solve the problem or alleviate the psychic distress. Saying and telling in psychology and the spiritual life equates to healing.

Taking this a step further, Genesis 2:18 can also apply to friendship. It is not good for a person to be without friends because friendship is a universal human need and a gift of the highest order. This applies even to the Lord in his human nature, as friendship is a need and a gift for him as much as it is for us.

In Sirach we read:

> Faithful friends are a sturdy shelter;
>> whoever finds one finds a treasure.
> Faithful friends are beyond price,
>> no amount can balance their worth. (6:14–15)

~

The word *fear* in Scripture in reference to God means reverential respect that prompts awe and obedience. Those who fear God, who genuinely respect and obey him are usually good people at heart and try to live in accord with the Gospel. They obey the commandments, and most of all the two Great Commandments which are the summation of the whole Christian life. They are people who share to some degree in God's life and holiness. People who fear the Lord make true friends. Again in Sirach we read:

> Those who fear the Lord enjoy stable friendship,
>> for as they are, so will their neighbors be. (6:17)

The second part of this verse refers to the idea that we become like the company we keep (Proverbs 13:20, 1 Corinthians 15:33). This points to our malleable nature as creatures and that we are shaped for good or ill partly through social conditioning and environmental factors.

The divine nature, on the other hand, is unchanging, and that is a good thing considering some of the company Jesus kept during his earthly life. He came to call sinners, not the righteous (Mark 2:17), and to call sinners means to associate with them and even to form friendships with them. In Luke, we read:

> For John the Baptist came neither eating food nor drinking wine, and you said, "He is possessed by a demon." The Son of Man came eating and drinking and you said, "Look, he is a glutton and a drunkard, a friend of tax collectors and sinners." (7:33–34)

Jesus is a friend of tax collectors and sinners but he does not become like them. The friendship he extends is meant to enable them to become more like him and eventually to make them saints, and if possible, hero-saints. Christ offers his companionship to tax collectors and sinners so that one day they might be able to reciprocate God's friendship.

All of us are called to friendship with God, and when we consider the matter, is there any higher vocation or mission than to be a true friend of God in this life and the next?

True Friendship and Christian Companionship

Moral Virtue	Intellectual Virtue
Good will	Content-oriented
Effective charity	Substance
Altruism	Learning
Shared togetherness	Knowledge
Sense of belonging	Truth
Mutual help and support	Understanding
Beneficence	Wisdom
Trust (the foundation of all	Prudence
human relationships)	Intelligence

False Friendship and Non-Christian Companionship

Moral Vice	Intellectual Vice
Ill will	Triviality
Malice	Frivolity
Maleficence	Vacuity
Egoism	Superficiality
Narcissism	Senselessness
Selfishness	Emptiness
Antipathy	Vanity
Antagonism	Sensuality
Isolation	Hedonism
Loneliness	Lies and deceit
Mistrust	Unreasonableness

16

A Primer on the Spiritual Life, Part 4

Much ink has been spilled trying to provide an adequate explanation for the existence of evil in the world, as if such an account could relieve at least some of the anxiety and grief humanity experiences because of it. In the spiritual life, we distinguish between moral evil, which is evil committed by rational beings (humans and angels) and includes some type of moral fault; and natural evil, which occurs in the natural world and includes such disasters as hurricanes, tornadoes, and volcanoes. The latter fall to the sciences to explain while the former is in the province of religion, philosophy, and law.

Remember that the Greek philosophers of the ancient world taught that evil is a privation of a good that should be there but is absent. The missing good, according to the Christian spiritual tradition, is grace and virtue, so the existence of moral evil in the world depends on whether human persons choose vice over virtue and God's will over self-will. The seat of individual choice is located in free will which has the capacity to choose between good and evil. The substance of the Christian answer to the problem of evil in the world has always been that God endowed every human person with free will and that evil exists in the world because people choose it.

Genius, as Einstein said, is making complex things simple, yet this answer does not fully satisfy our need to know why evil exists in the world. Free will is a faculty of choice, but it does not explain how we choose or why we choose. The answer to this conundrum is complex and will forever be a subject of research and speculation in the psychological sciences and spirituality, but a concise explanation can be found in Christian theology:

Spiritual Principle #12: The will always chooses the good.

The good here is not necessarily the true good. The faculty of the intellect identifies what it *believes* to be the good through cognition, but the human intellect is as prone to error as the human will. The distinction here is between the authentic good and a perceived good, or one that *appears* to the intellect to be good but is actually specious and deceptive. The will acts on this determination of the intellect and always chooses what it perceives to be the good, even if it is a false good. Perception always precedes judgment. So when people choose vice and evil, they do so because they perceive some good in it, even if it is only a specious or selfish good.

So how are the will and intellect deceived? While the psychological sciences offer a wealth of knowledge on this subject, three reasons are prominent from the perspective of the spiritual life: (1) the passions, (2) the improper use of human reason, or poor decision-making, and (3) the habit of wrongdoing and sin.

The word *passion* is defined as: (1) a strong feeling or emotion, (2) a strong interest or desire, and (3) a time of intense suffering, usually referring to Christ's Passion but sometimes to saints and holy people who suffer in union with and in imitation of Jesus. As a feeling or desire, the passions are neutral in themselves but can be directed toward virtuous or vicious ends. In Christian spiritual literature, the word *passion* is often used in the pejorative sense and involves being unusually attached to something. A scriptural example of this usage comes from Saint Paul when he refers to the selfish and unreasonable passions and desires of the flesh (Galatians 5:24).

The passion of hate is a particularly thorny one to understand. It works in coordination with the passion of love. Love draws the will to what the intellect perceives to be the good, while hate causes an aversion to what the intellect perceives to be evil. What does it mean in the Bible when it says that God "hates" something or when "hate" or a similar sentiment is attributed to one of the patriarchs, prophets, or another biblical personage? Commentaries on Sacred Scripture define *hate* in the Bible as the preference for one thing over another, so if Scripture says that God "hates evil," it is to be interpreted in the sense that he prefers good over evil. Some Bible translations state that Jacob hated Leah and loved Rachel, which means that he preferred Rachel over Leah as a wife and showed her more favor since he loved her more. (Genesis 29:30–31)

As a matter of scriptural hermeneutics, the word *hate* is therefore not always used in the Bible as it is commonly used in English, that is, with a negative, even malicious connotation. It is true when we experience hate externalized, and especially when it is coupled with anger, it is almost always vicious, but when kept in check and oriented toward the true good, it can be directed toward virtuous ends. Hate as a passion in the neutral sense is a constituent part of human nature created by God to aid humans in rejecting one thing in preference to another. It is inconvenient and somewhat a shame that the same word in English is used both in reference to malice and to a natural part of the human person.

In the second sense, the word *passion* can be used as a strong interest or desire. I might have an interest in baseball, which is not morally objectionable, but if I become so strongly attached to it that it causes me to do wrong or sin, then it has become a passion. Games of chance are not morally objectionable if engaged in moderately and on a recreational basis, but if my gambling habit has become so deeply ingrained that it develops into an addiction, then I have become attached to it and it may very well be sinful.

Spiritual Principle #13: All sin involves an unhealthy attachment to creatures.

The second reason the will and intellect are deceived (i.e., the improper use of human reason, or poor decision-making) often involves the passions. In the New Testament we read about the selfish and unreasonable passions and desires of the flesh (Galatians 5:24), and with a little consideration and some empirical evidence, it is clear how selfish and unreasonable human beings can be.

The third reason is that the habit of sin and wrongdoing darkens and corrupts the mind making it more difficult to discern what is truly good and what is specious and harmful. Repeated bad acts represent a threat to spiritual health because they deform the conscience and distort moral character. In the Acts of the Apostles, the scales that fell from Saint Paul's eyes when Ananias laid hands on him were a sign of physical and spiritual blindness (Acts 9:17–18). In similar fashion, sin spiritually wounds the soul just as physical wounds are suffered in the body. The choice of evil harms others, but it harms the sinner as much if not more.

> **Spiritual Principle #14**: All rebellion leads to death. The
> wages of sin is death (Romans 6:23).

The remedy for the existence of evil in the world is obedience to God's will, the practice of moral and intellectual virtue, sound decision-making, right-mindedness, and right judgment. The basis of good decision-making is the correct use of human reason.

Modern culture often transmits messages that conflict with traditional Christian teaching on the spiritual life. One is that human sensibilities and emotions are an acceptable basis for making moral decisions. Christian tradition, on the other hand, does not recommend the sensibilities and emotions as a sound basis for moral decision-making. This tradition and a little self-reflection remind us that there are plenty of examples in the lives of most of us when sensibilities and emotions have shown themselves to be notoriously untrustworthy.

Reason enlightened by grace is to be vastly preferred. The habit of prayer goes a long way in obtaining grace, and a little study of logic is helpful in improving one's faculty of reason. In addition, the psychological sciences offer a wealth of useful information. For instance, researchers have found that expert problem solvers have three key advantages over novice problem solvers: (1) they employ solution principles rather than rely on surface characteristics, (2) they reason forward from premises to conclusions rather than working backward from preconceived ideas, and (3) they use chunking, which refers to the memory's ability to group bits of knowledge together.

It is also useful to distinguish between absolute certitude and moral certitude. There was a time when mathematicians believed that Newtonian mathematics applied to everything in the universe, but mathematicians and physicists in the twentieth century, notably Einstein, altered that view. There are in fact few things in life we can be absolutely certain of, and the bar for absolute certainty is set very high. Moral certainty, on the other hand, is a less difficult standard to attain. After a period of reflection and examination and all things being considered, if the evidence points in a certain direction, then I may attain a level of moral certainty about the matter under consideration. I may not be absolutely certain, but I can be morally sure about the truth or falsity of a claim, or the rightness or wrongness of an action.

If it is difficult to apply the standard of absolute certainty to physical reality, then it is even more problematic when considering metaphysical reality. In order to have a conversation about theology, it is necessary to agree on the existence of three things which cannot be proved using human reason alone but must be accepted in faith: God, the immortal human soul, and an afterlife. The standard of moral certainty is much easier to apply to these, as everything in life convinces me of their existence.

17

The Path of Life

BelCap and TimTop stood at the beginning of the Path of Life.

Being of the same age, they schooled together, became friends, played baseball and football together, and went on double dates when they were in high school.

As they prepared to go their separate ways, they came to a fork in the road. On the left they saw a wide path paved with flowers, ornamental shrubbery, and fruit trees. A sign at the beginning of the path read, "Ease and Comfort." Another sign read, "Delight to the Eyes." A third sign read, "The Way is Wide and Narrow."

BelCap wondered at the meaning of the third sign.

There was a man standing at the entrance to the path on the left. He was handsome, one of the beautiful people, and dressed in a fine suit with a scarlet tie and a crimson carnation in his lapel. He smiled in a welcoming manner. His name was Abaddon.

On the right there was a narrow gate. On it were signs that read, "Christ" and "True Discipleship." Standing to the side of the gate was a man dressed in a shabby, worn-out robe. His hair was disheveled, his beard unkempt. He was wearing sandals and looked the kind of person who would ask wayfarers for money, one of those down on his luck with not much going for him.

TimTop wondered at the man at the gate.

BelCap turned to TimTop and wished him well on his journey. They agreed they would see each other again someday.

BelCap turned to the left and the man Abaddon smiled more widely. BelCap began to walk toward the path and noticed it was wide and flat and easy to walk on. Granite stones lined the path on both sides and the grass around the pavers was trimmed. The trees bore low-hanging fruit that appeared to be good to eat. He felt confident that this was a good choice.

TimTop approached the man in the tattered, dusty robe and wondered if he was going to ask for money. The man looked and smelled as if he had been on a long journey. Dusty in appearance, he seemed like he needed a good meal and a place to sleep. As TimTop approached nearer to the gate, the man unlatched it and pulled it open. Without saying a word, TimTop walked through the gate onto a narrow path.

As BelCap made his way along his journey, he began to see more signs like the ones at the fork in the road. Some had arrows pointing left or right, others did not. The signs read, "Sloth," "Envy," "Pride," and "Lust." He ignored them and continued on his journey.

As TimTop walked for some time down the narrow path, he too began to see signs that read, "Labor," "Hardship," "Patience," and "Good Will." Wondering if he had made the right decision, he thought of BelCap and how he was faring. Further along, he saw signs marked, "Faith," "Hope," and "Prudence." Feeling somewhat consoled, he decided to continue and wondered if the man in the shabby robe were still waiting at the gate.

As months turned into years, BelCap passed many milestones in life. He married and began raising a family. Along the road were signs that read, "Greed," "Superficiality," "Frivolity," and "Vanity." He remembered having committed a few small faults from time to time along the way, and there was that little affair with the young woman before she moved out of town, but BelCap was generally liked by his peers and was making a good living.

TimTop also married and was usefully employed. The path he chose became narrower at times. At various points he passed signs marked, "Long-Suffering," "Patient Endurance," "Justice," and "Fortitude." Once he passed a sign that read, "Way of the Cross." He never forgot about the man in the shabby robe.

Many years passed, and BelCap's children had grown and left home. He was still married to his wife, but they were unhappy. Along the path, BelCap passed signs that read, "Greed," "Anger," and "Gluttony." He remembered times when he became unnecessarily irate with his wife and children. He had eaten and drank too much and it showed. At one point, BelCap was embezzling from his employer—small amounts that nobody would easily notice. Then he began to sense from his coworkers that they were catching on, so he applied for another job and was hired. As he continued to walk along the path, he noticed the trees bore less and less fruit until finally they bore nothing but leaves. The flowers that once lined the path were long gone, and on the ground where grass had once grown were now leaves and other signs of autumn. The pavers were no more, and it was easier to wander from the path. Sometimes he did, only to return disappointed.

TimTop's children had also grown and left home to start their own families. His path led him to a desert area marked "Self-Denial," "The Holy Cross," "Purification," and "Temperance." At times he became dejected, especially when the signs of "Tribulation" and "Trial" appeared, but there were other times when he was encouraged by signs that read, "Reward," "Fulfillment," and "Satisfaction." TimTop never regretted having chosen this path.

In his later years, BelCap enjoyed some measure of wealth, but the path he was on became more desolate and narrow. The trees were of the deciduous variety in winter, and once in a while he thought he saw what might have been a locust. On one occasion, he noticed a scorpion on the path which he neatly avoided. The few slugs and snails he came upon, he stepped on. Signs he passed read, "Selfishness," "Arrogance," and "Self-Love." At one point during his journey, he came upon a "Defile" which he only slightly avoided.

TimTop retired and was slowly growing old. As he looked back on his life, he remembered passing through times of "Humiliation" and "Sacrifice," "Trust in God" and "Self-Control." He and his wife were still happily married and were helping to raise their grandchildren. The signs on the path at this time in his life read, "Service," "Benevolence," "Lights," and "Counsels." He never looked back in regret.

As BelCap was approaching the end of his earthly life, he came upon a man standing beside a gate. There was another man standing along the path about twenty feet before the gate, and a sign beside him read, "Manipulation and Deceit." Both men were wearing soiled robes. Beside the gate was a sign that read, "The Land of Desolation." The man at the gate grinned slightly and glared at BelCap. His name was Apollyon. Despite these omens, a sense of calm came over BelCap, the kind one feels when a storm is on the horizon. He knew his time had come.

The man called Apollyon did not open the gate. That was not his job. He and BelCap waited for a moment while the other man looked on. The gate opened on its own, and BelCap stepped toward the gate. As he passed the man called Apollyon, he noticed a mild odor that reminded him of a reptile or a bag of mealworms. Apollyon grinned.

TimTop was also approaching the end of his life and passed signs that read, "Charity" and "Virtue." He came upon a man standing before a sign marked, "Guardian and Guide." TimTop was comforted. Further along he saw another sign that read, "The Land of the Living."

TimTop knew his life journey was coming to a close, and as he endured his final illness, he saw signs marked, "Tolerance" and "Forbearance." The final sign he remembered seeing before he fell asleep was "Perfect Charity."

As BelCap passed through the gate, he lost consciousness. When he awoke, he was blinded by a darkness as if he had never in his life possessed the sense of sight. It was darker than any night sky, the complete absence of light or anything else. Behind him he heard a deep, husky voice, clear and ominous … "Huh, huh, huh, huh, huh…" Ahead of him he sensed that something was observing him, but he did not know for sure. Suddenly, the floor seemed to vanish beneath his feet and he felt himself begin to fall as if into a chasm. The last thing he remembered was screaming: "I WANT TO LIVE! I WANT TO LIVE!!"

When TimTop awoke, he was in a garden filled with the most beautiful flowers he had ever seen. Before his mind flashed all the scenes of his life. In front of him on the other side of the garden was a Being of Light from whom emanated warmth and benevolence. TimTop felt welcomed, as if he were meant to be there at that very moment, as if the Being of Light were waiting for him for a very long time. TimTop realized this was his time of reckoning…

Neither of them spoke audibly, but TimTop became aware that the Being of Light was asking him a question. It was not an audible question, but more like an impression which filled TimTop's whole being. It was the only thing he could think of at the moment:

"What did you do with the Love that I gave you?"

As he was reviewing the scenes of his life in his mind, TimTop thought for a moment. With some sorrow and hesitation he was about to speak, but before he could, a voice from deep within his breast, clear and distinct as if from his very core, said:

"I did the best I could."

A Spiritual Map

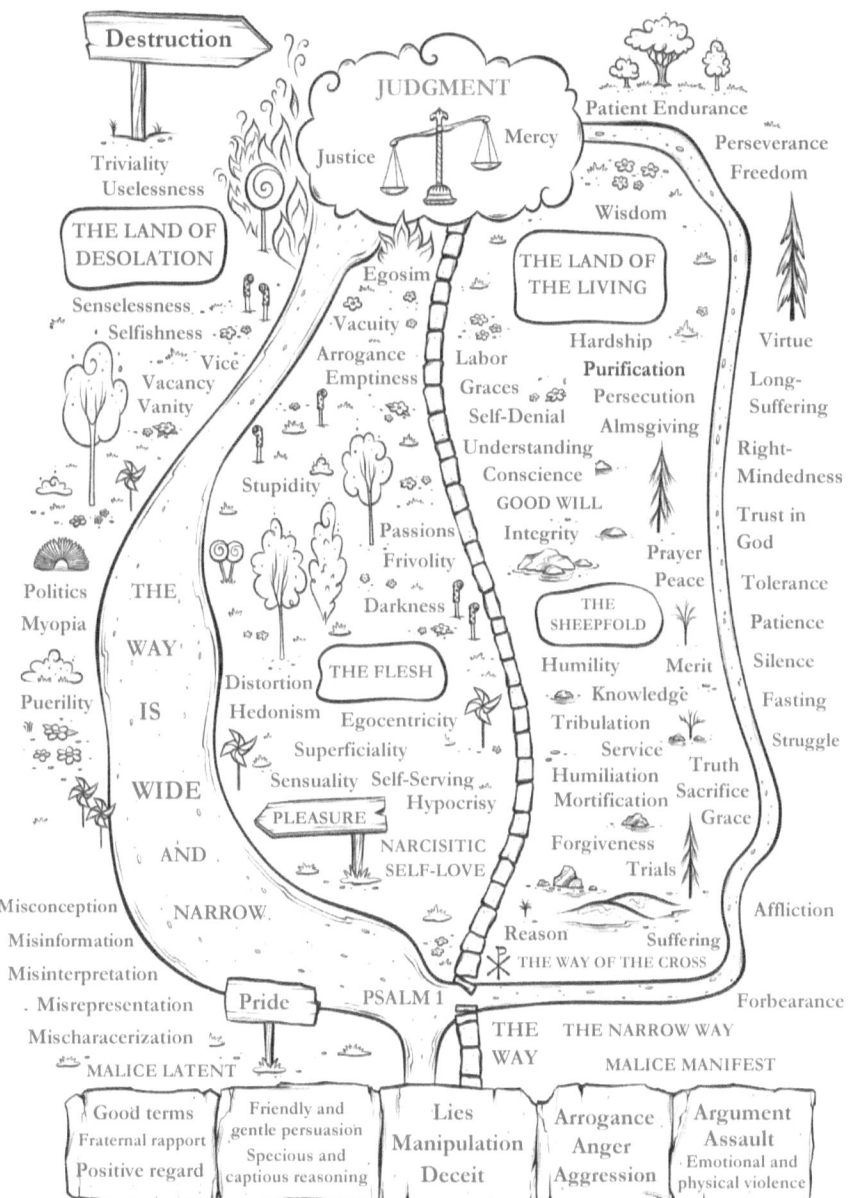

18

The B.A. Principle

A useful principle in theology and the spiritual life is one I call the B.A. Principle, otherwise known as the "Both–And" or "But–Also" Principle. It allows one to hold in one's mind two seemingly irreconcilable and even contradictory aspects of a physical or metaphysical reality. The key to its successful usage is the application of balance and good will with regard to interpretation.

The B.A. Principle is germane but not limited to the following Christian doctrine:

a) The Holy Trinity is three divine Persons and one God.

b) God is *both* three *and* one.

c) God is three, *but* he is *also* one.

• • •

a) Jesus Christ is one divine Person with two natures, divine and human.

b) The divine Person of Jesus Christ possesses *both* a divine nature *and* a human nature.

c) The Person of Christ has a divine nature, *but* he *also* has a human nature.

. . .

a) The Christian Church is of this world and the next.

b) The Church is *both* temporal and earthly, *and* spiritual, celestial, and eternal.

c) The Church is temporal and earthly, *but* it is *also* spiritual, celestial, and eternal.

. . .

a) The Church is human and divine.

b) The Church has *both* a human element *and* a divine element.

c) The Church is human, *but* it is *also* divine.

. . .

a) There is worldliness and division within the Church, yet there is also holiness and unity.

b) The Church is *both* worldly and divided, *and* at the same time holy and one.

c) The Church is worldly and divided, *but* there is *also* holiness and unity within it.

. . .

a) Scripture is the Word of God in human words.
b) Scripture is *both* the inspired Word of God *and* a collection of historical documents.
c) Scripture is inspired, *but* it is *also* a composition of human writings that took centuries to compile and involved a great deal of human effort and ingenuity.

• • •

a) The human person is body and soul.
b) The human person is composed of *both* a spiritual principle we call a soul *and* a corporal substance which we call a body
c) The human person has a body, *but* he or she *also* has a soul.

• • •

a) The human person is mortal and eternal.
b) The human person is *both* mortal with regard to this life *and* eternal with regard to the next.
c) Human beings are mortal, *but* we are *also* eternal.

• • •

One of the ways heresy has arisen in the Church is that it emphasizes some measure of the truth of one aspect of a physical or metaphysical reality and the attenuation of the truth of the other. There are certainly degrees of importance between the two sides of the B.A. Principle (e.g., divinity is more important than humanity), but both sides remain nonetheless true.

A useful image to employ here is a seesaw. One of the most important things in life is balance, and even more important is good will. We try to keep the seesaw in balance even if there are degrees of importance, and we use good will to interpret not according to our own will and preferences, but in keeping with accepted Christian doctrine.

19

Binary Movements and Decisions

As stated earlier, the binary decision all computers make at their core is the decision between 1 and 0. All of the computations made by computers flow from this foundational core decision.

Human beings also have a core which we call the *heart*. It is the center of our being, the deepest level of our human being-ness. Human persons are not computers, however, and despite the vast computational power of today's modern machines and their almost infinite potential, computers will never possess a human heart and spirit. We are more than a binary choice, and grace is not imparted to computers. Computers are more complex than humans in some ways, but not all. Computers have their own form of complexity, just as human beings have the faculties of will and intellect that make us complex in ways that computers will never be despite the ongoing debate of whether or not they will ever gain consciousness.

Just as all analogies and metaphors fail, the reduction of the human person to a binary mechanism and the diminution of his or her spiritual movements and rational decisions to a binary system will ultimately fail. Nevertheless, even as Psalm 1 is a simplification—there are two ways a person can choose, the high road or the low road, and there are two final and eternal destinations, heaven and hell—this simplification is nevertheless true and helpful. In the same manner, the human heart, mind, and will are important objects of study in the spiritual life however irreducible they are, and it is useful to give an account of their binary aspects even if that account is a simplification. Einstein, who grasped the intricacies of mathematics as well as anyone, said that if we cannot explain something in simple terms, then we do not truly understand it.

First spiritual movement of the human heart

The first movement of the human heart is always love, which is an ambiguous and variable word in English. A spiritual *movement* is not the same as a conscious, rational *decision* taken through discursive and intuitive reasoning. The first movement of love is a spiritual movement or impulse that emanates from deep within us and is not entirely under our conscious control or subject to an immediate decision-making process. We may respond to it, however, after the movement or impulse has occurred through interior or exterior acts, and over time it may strengthen or diminish. Grace also may influence it, but always for the purpose of bringing us closer to God and to help us to attain salvation. *Formation* is the term we use for the continual process that occurs over time whereby our acts, internal and external, interact with divine grace if it is, in fact, being imparted.

Spiritual love always reaches beyond itself toward an object outside of itself. It has a preference for and selects an object we call the good, whether that good is real (true, actual) or perceived (imaginary, false). Our heart spiritually loves what it identifies as a good and hates what it identifies as evil, bad, inferior, or in some way defective.

A problem arises because the words *love*, *hate*, *good*, and *bad* are relative and uncertain in meaning. Some Bible translations use the word *hate* when another word or phrase would be better suited, but publishers want their translations to read elegantly and opt against words or phrases that sound clunky, unnatural, or are otherwise not according to common usage. Since elegance is not my top priority, I have here the luxury of using other words to avoid the negative connotations that come with the word *hate*.

First Binary Movement of the Human Heart

Love	Hate
Affection	Disaffection
Attraction	Repulsion
Inclination	Disinclination
Preference	Disfavor
Predilection	Un-love

It is important to note that the first movement of the human heart is inconstant, variable, changeable, even whimsical, and sometimes surprises us. We do not often reflect on the immediate impulse the moment it happens, but it is available for introspection. Even so, we usually just react to it and move on.

Our heart has a mind of its own, so to speak, and we cannot change it overnight or by a mere act of the will or through reasoning. Some impulses and desires are particularly difficult to move beyond, as when we love someone who does not reciprocate our love or desire something which we cannot have. If the impulse is strong enough, we can become disillusioned, saddened, envious, and sometimes react in a way that is unloving and even hateful.

Second spiritual movement of the human heart

The second movement of the human heart is the movement between interest and disinterest. When we look inside ourselves, we find that we are interested in this item and disinterested in that one. I do not assert that this second movement follows chronologically from the first or that the will and intellect play no part in our interests or disinterests. I only suggest that the second movement proceeds along with or after the first and that it comes from deep within us.

The natural impulse of interest and disinterest has a spontaneous manner to it. We cannot always determine who or what interests or disinterests us. We find this movement is automatic rather than volitional. We meet people who are of immediate interest to us and others who are of little or no interest. Some people discover in their youth that they are interested in a particular field of study or profession even if they can hardly explain why that interest exists.

We notice as we progress through life that our interests and disinterests ebb and change. Sometimes we lose interest in something that once fascinated us, and at other times we gain an interest in what formerly bored and wearied us. We find that some interests deepen and strengthen over time and disinterests become aversions. All of this happens in a way that is to some extent outside of our control. The heart has a mind of its own.

Third spiritual movement of the human heart

The third movement of the human heart that proceeds along with the first two is between acceptance/approval and rejection/disapproval. Like the other two, this movement is both powerful and potentially dangerous. The ultimate object of our love must always be God since he designed our nature to be this way, and all sin involves an unhealthy attachment to creatures. This must be accepted as a priori and requires that we love and accept what comes from God, and disapprove of and reject what is contrary to his will.

This is why prayer, living the spiritual life, and introspection are necessary for spiritual growth and salvation. If we look within ourselves and find movements or, God forbid, habitual dispositions that are contrary to our ultimate good, then we must counter them by conscious decisions and acts of our free will. If we find that our heart is aligned with our ultimate good, we can count it as a work of grace and consider it the greatest blessing. If not, then we have work to do.

All of this to say that we are not predetermined by what proceeds from the heart. The will and intellect always have their part to play for most of us, and we remain free even if we are something of a mystery to ourselves. Acts form habits and habits form dispositions. We have input into the formation of our deepest selves and are not determined by the movements that arise from our heart even if we cannot escape them. What we do in response to these movements, however, is a reaction to them as an affirmation or denial.

Binary decision of the will aided by the intellect

The will operates on a more conscious and rational basis than spiritual love that arises from the heart, but it also has a binary characteristic. The will always chooses the good and rejects the bad. Even if the decision-making process is more conscious and deliberate than the spiritual movements of the heart, our power to choose the good is neither absolute nor ever entirely deficient, except for possibly the insane. Freedom is defined as the power to choose the good, but we are free only to a greater or lesser degree. The more virtuous we are, the freer we are to choose the true good. The more habituated we are in vice, the less power we have to choose the true good.

Ill will is the demonstration of the power to choose the false good, but it is nonetheless a power. Human beings have an innate need to exercise power in some form, and those who exercise ill will are satisfying this need in a way that is harmful to themselves and others. Much evil is accomplished in this world because of ill will and there is no denying its power. Good will, on the other hand, is often associated with weakness because those who practice it limit or deny themselves the option of hurting others and yet remain subject to ill will. This state of affairs is limited to this temporal world, however, and there is always a future, and the future is eternal, and there is a God who rewards and punishes.

Binary Decision of the Will

Love	Hate
Good will	Ill will
Beneficence	Maleficence
Altruism	Selfishness
Charity	Egoism
Virtue	Vice

The fundamental principle of all history is the conflict between good and evil, and the most important and perennial decision we make throughout our lives is the choice between good and evil, good will and ill will. All human interaction, society, and history are influenced and shaped by this binary decision in a manner analogous to the computations of computers which result from the choice between 1 and 0. A lifetime of good will eventually leads to a wealth of 1s which we call merit. A lifetime of ill will eventually ends in a bankruptcy of 0s. When we finally arrive at our individual judgment at the end of our mortal life, we will see the deposit we made from our good will and the debt we incurred from our ill will.

Relationships are the most important priority in life. Those that foster mutual affection, interest, acceptance, and good will survive and grow into meaningful and supportive friendships and charitable acquaintanceships. Those in which disaffection, disinterest, rejection, and ill will thrive will inevitably result in strife and enmity. People who have lived in prison say there are no friends in prison. Is there any reason to believe there are friends in hell?

20

Scripture and History

We must be careful about learning history from the Bible just as we must be careful about learning science from the Bible. Scripture is a collection of historical documents and many of the books serve as invaluable historical sources for professional research and study, but it is not a history book in the ordinary sense, just as it is not a science book in the ordinary sense, even if it describes an ancient cosmology.

Our sources of history (i.e., extant written documents) are notoriously unreliable when it comes to facts. This is true not only for ancient documents, but also for those from the medieval period and into the early modern age. To be interpreted properly, like any other historical source, the books of the Bible must be compared with other contemporary or near-contemporary documents which often give a different portrayal of events. Also to be considered are archaeological finds, anthropological discoveries, theological doctrine, reasonable speculation, the conjecture of historians, and common sense.

We must also be careful about how literally we interpret Scripture just as we are careful about how literally we interpret other ancient writings. It is true that Scripture is in a class by itself when it comes to divine inspiration, but it is not entirely distinct from all ancient writings in other respects. The Bible was written by human authors just as other ancient writings were, and the ancient Hebrews who wrote the Old Testament and the Jewish Christians who wrote the New Testament, like all ancient peoples, had a purpose for writing that we must be aware of when we approach those texts today. This awareness requires study.

Ancient authors were not always trying to give a factual account of what actually happened, and much of their writing was not factual at all. Ancient civilizations produced fictional works of literature just as modern societies do. Even if the ancients were attempting to give a factual account, fact often got mixed in with fiction:

- The Israelites, Greeks, Romans, and other peoples of antiquity crafted stories, legends, and myths to give themselves a communal identity and to explain their origin and the reason for the existence of their tribe, city-state, kingdom, empire, etc. Public storytelling also served as a form of entertainment much like our theater, TV, and radio.

- Homer (if there was a Homer) wrote the *Iliad* and the *Odyssey* to give an account of the origins and early history of the Greek peoples, but no one believes these accounts are actual history even if they might be based on actual historical events. We recognize these stories as myth passed down orally from generation to generation, renditions of it recited around campfires or in open-air theaters until someone finally put it in writing. That process took generations and the story was surely changed and embellished any number of times. No one believes it is historical fact, just literature with a purpose.

- The Greeks had their pantheon of gods in part to explain natural phenomena for which we have scientific explanations. No one believes any of it actually happened, and even in those days there were plenty of skeptics and atheists (see Plato, Aristotle, and other Greek philosophers).

- Scripture also began as an oral tradition and was passed down with modifications from generation to generation until scribes finally put it in writing. Those papyrus or parchment scrolls were then passed down and copied (with mistakes, redactions, additions, deletions, embellishments, etc.) until they were so old they fell apart or rotted, and new copies were made (with liberties taken) such that we have no original copies of any of the books of the Bible, even if we have ancient sources (Hebrew Scriptures, Dead Sea Scrolls, New Testament writings). The miracle of grace is that throughout this whole process, God was inspiring, teaching, and guiding those scribes and communicating truths that lead to salvation. God's inspiration is the leaven of truth and Word of God in Scripture in a way that it is not in other forms of literature, ancient or modern. Nevertheless, those documents are still human writings. (See the B.A. Principle.)

- Virgil wrote the *Aeneid* during the reign of Caesar Augustus to give an account of the origins of Rome and invented a story in which the city of Troy serves as the origin of the city of Rome, but no one believes it is actual history. Even in Roman times, people understood it was a well-crafted piece of literature that served as an origin and identity story that was much more impressive than the real history of an entirely insignificant Latin tribe that emerged from the swampy ground around the Tiber.

- *Beowulf* was written during the Middle Ages as a hero-tale that provided the people of Anglo-Saxon England with an epic account of a hero who gave them a sense of identity and history. It too probably developed as an oral tradition and then finally someone put it in writing. No one believes it is historically true, but it served an important purpose for the Anglo-Saxons who, like all other human beings, needed to have an identity rooted in the past.

- The Scandinavians created Norse mythology, but no one believes it is history, just literature with a purpose.

- The original stories of King Arthur and the Knights of the Round Table are good literature (if you enjoy reading Arthurian legend) and they give an account of the almost ideal medieval king and kingdom, but no one believes it is history—just a nice story that was written to teach how a medieval king and his nobles should act within an ideal medieval society, even if some of its members had moral flaws.

I hesitate to include Scripture in the above list because it is truly in a class all its own as the "Word of God in human words," but it is important to keep in mind that it was originally written for ancient Semitic tribes, sometimes nomadic, who had a theocratic worldview and form of governance. These sacred writings provided a common religious and political identity and served as a means of salvation for a people who lived in dangerous, unpredictable times—"somehow God is going to rescue us/me." The understanding we have of salvation today took many centuries to develop, however. The ancient belief in Hades has long been abandoned, and even in Jesus' time, the Sadducees did not believe in the Resurrection.

If you want to believe literally in the Genesis story of creation, you are free to do so, but science has shown something else actually happened. If you want to believe the whole story of the Exodus, you are free to do so, but there are other theories as to how that migration out of Egypt took place. If you want to believe in the miracles and plagues of Moses and Aaron, you may freely do so, but the study of history shows that God did not work such dramatic miracles during other periods of history, not even for the Jews when they were being persecuted over centuries.

The New Testament is considered more historically reliable than the Old Testament because it was written in the first century AD. Nevertheless, it has to be professionally interpreted using the same hermeneutical principles as the Old Testament when it comes to history. (For a good source of hermeneutical principles, see *The New Jerome Biblical Commentary.*) It is important that lay, unstudied persons rely on the work of scholars and biblical commentators who spend their academic and religious lives studying these ancient documents and not on their own views and subjective interpretations. Even when it comes to spirituality in the Bible, interpretation is best left to the well-informed.

~

In summary, the important points to know are:

(1) The two key principles always to remember when it comes to Scripture are: (a) interpretation is crucial, and (b) all translations are interpretations.

(2) Scripture is not a history book, nor is it a science book, a psychology book, a book of literature, or any kind of work properly classified in any academic subject area except Scripture study, theology, and religion.

(3) The Bible is a library of books that for us teach spiritual truths that lead to salvation. Some of its books are fictional works (Job, Tobit, Esther), yet fiction can teach truth. There are also nonfiction books (Gospels, New Testament writings), but we

have to be careful about how literally we view these accounts and letters. Nonfiction may not necessarily be entirely factual, just as fiction is not necessarily false.

(4) We use Scripture today somewhat differently than did the ancients. Scripture is for us a historical source of our Judeo-Christian heritage, and it serves as a guide to salvation that needs to be properly interpreted. The Hebrews of the Old Testament sought after salvation, but their understanding of it differed from the New Testament Christian Jews, and there has been a further development of doctrine since the first century AD.

~

None of the preceding should disillusion anyone. The authors of Scripture were, above all, human beings living human lives, and it is very unlikely they experienced supernatural phenomena in a manner different from how we experience it. It might not hurt your chances of salvation to believe in the Bible as a literal source of history, but it is safe to assume that God dealt with people in every age in the same way he deals with us. The Red Sea was almost certainly not parted as depicted in the movie *The Ten Commandments*. It is indisputable that God works miracles at times, but they are usually if not always on the subtle side. God can be found in the still, small voice (1 Kings 19:12). He does not seem to be much of a showman.

At least not on this side of eternity.

21

A Primer on the Spiritual Life, Part 5

Suffering is a problematic topic to address. No matter what one says, it is difficult to make it sound appealing or even tolerable, if that is at all possible. It is also difficult to convince most people that personal holiness is an immense good that should be pursued because people are generally lazy about spiritual things and they intuitively know that holiness requires sacrifice and suffering.

The path to holiness always involves:

1. Sacrifice—what we give up of our own volition

2. Suffering—comes to us whether we pursue holiness or not

3. Loss—what is taken away from us either as a natural part of life or by God for our greater good.

Spiritual Principle #15: You have to give up something to get something.

If we are expected to accept suffering for the sake of our spiritual profit, it is helpful to know a little about the nature of suffering. Saint Paul talks about two forms of suffering: one that leads to righteousness and the other to death. The second kind that leads to death we see in wrongdoers who refuse to repent and thus prevent themselves from receiving God's grace. This kind of suffering can lead in the worst cases to the disintegration of the personality and severe mental illness. (This is not to say that all people with mental illness, even severe types, are sinners.) For people who do not manifest signs of disintegration or mental illness, Saint John Vianney reminds us that even worldly people have their cross to bear, and every cross entails some form of suffering. There are "crosses" that do not lead to heaven, but they still involve suffering. This is what Saint Paul means when he addresses the kind of suffering that leads to death. There is no redemption or reward on the other side of it.

Nevertheless, these kinds of crosses may still be of benefit and God permits worldly suffering for the sake of some spiritual good. Remember that God's object is always the salvation of the soul, not its death. He permits suffering because it can be a sign to us that we are doing something wrong in life, and some people only learn through suffering because they simply do not respond to counsel, admonition, or example. There are drug addicts, for example, who go to clinics but are not ready for help because they have not hit rock bottom yet. It is only at that point that some people are ready for conversion and repentance and thus ready for the first kind of suffering that leads to righteousness, healing, and wholeness.

> **Spiritual Principle #16**: Embedded in every cross is at least one grace.

Suffering that leads to righteousness is a participation in the Cross of Christ and is most profitable to a soul because it has three important benefits in the spiritual life:

1. It purifies, cleanses, and heals the soul.

2. It detaches the soul from unhealthy attachment to created objects that have the potential to entice us to choose them over God's will.

3. It tames the soul and makes it docile and receptive to divine grace.

These three benefits are of immense importance and their value cannot be overstated. Although suffering is difficult and unwelcome, God attaches great reward to it, and it should be that way. Why should God give his best gifts for easy things? Normal human life rarely works that way. The best things in life require some form of effort, sacrifice, and suffering. The same holds true in the spiritual life. The best things in life are not easy and free, and the best things in the spiritual life also require effort and sacrifice. Our Lord revealed to Saint Faustina that he does not reward for good feelings and success, but for labor, hardship, patience, and good will. Just as sin carries within itself an inherent penalty that is not inflicted directly by God, so suffering brings its own intrinsic rewards, although God alone has power in the spiritual life to make these efficacious. "Without me you can do nothing" (John 15:5).

We find in the Christian tradition examples of saints and holy people who extol the benefits of suffering and teach that people would desire suffering if they only knew the true value of it. Saint Rose of Lima, for example, wrote:

> Let all men know that grace comes after tribulation. Let them know that without the burden of afflictions it is impossible to reach the height of grace. Let them know that the gifts of grace increase as the struggles increase... [W]ithout the cross they can find no road to climb to heaven... We cannot obtain grace unless we suffer afflictions... We must heap trouble upon trouble to attain a deep participation in the divine nature [holiness]... No one would complain about his cross or about troubles that may happen to him, if he would come to know the scales on which they are weighed when they are distributed to men.[4]

Francis de Sales also promoted the value of suffering in his counsel that we should live a living death and a dying life. This does not sound very appealing, but we must remember that he is teaching in light of the New Testament epistles which state that we must conform ourselves to the crucified Christ who "learned obedience from what he suffered" (Hebrews 5:8).

---

[4] "Memorial of Saint Rose of Lima," Office of Readings, August 23, *The Liturgy of the Hours,* vol. 4, (New York: Catholic Book Publishing Company, 1975), 1342-3.

While suffering is profitable in the spiritual life, Christian spiritual masters advise that we should never ask for it, even for the purpose of holiness or purification. They advise us instead to let God decide when to send trials and tribulations. He will always send the piece that fits at the right time if we are faithful. It is our job to be vigilant and do our best to comply with his will.

Spiritual Principle #17: Whatever one needs, God sends.

We find in the Christian literature a healthy and pragmatic way to view suffering, one that is encouraging and consoling. Saint Augustine, among many, reminds us that suffering is inevitable and that we may as well bear hardship in union with God's will and for our spiritual benefit:

> Our pilgrimage on earth cannot be exempt from trial. We progress by means of trial. No one knows himself except through trial, or receives a crown except after victories, or strives except against an enemy or temptations.[5]

---

[5] "First Sunday of Lent," Office of Readings, *The Liturgy of the Hours,* vol. 2, (New York: Catholic Book Publishing Company, 1975), 87.

How to Draw a Spiritual Battle Map

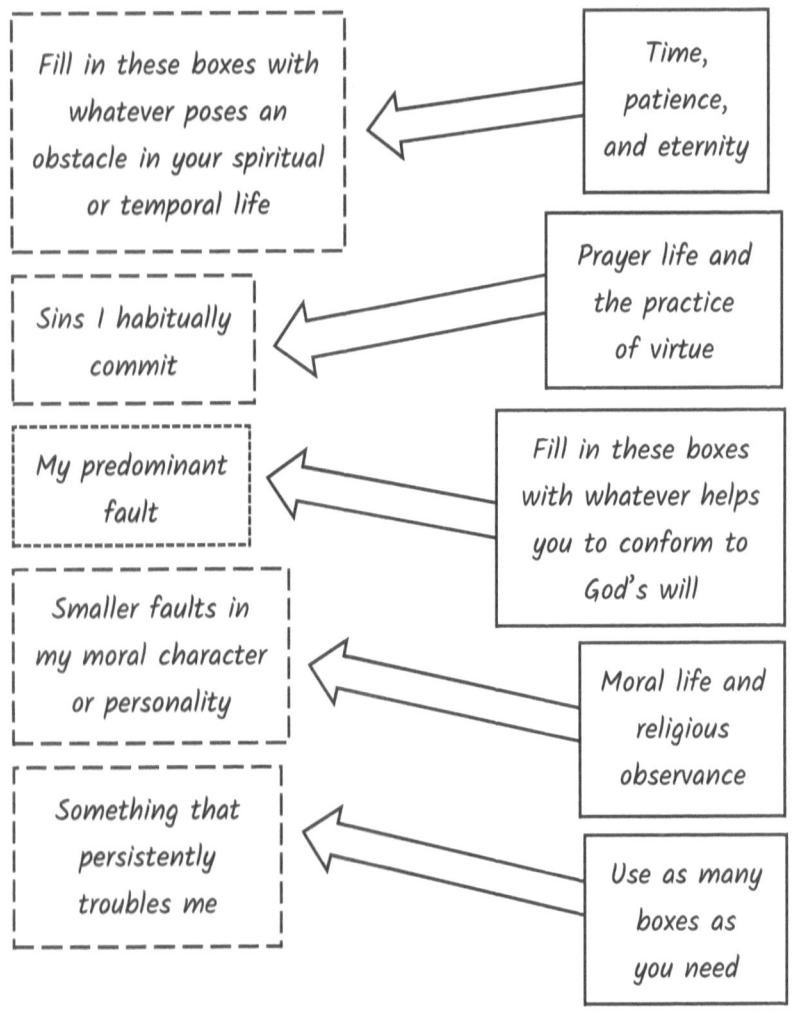

Spiritual Battle Map 20?? (Year)

22

Plenty of Time

In the infernal regions where dwell in hell
   Those eternal spirits who forever rebel
      Against all that is Good.

And on his chamber pot he sits
   The first dissenter against the Three
      On his sulfuric throne
        Alone
      As he would not otherwise have it.

Once he did call to his seat
   Those without feet
      Who cannot flee from him
   To canvass their opinion
      Of how he might increase his daily harvest.

"Tell me, drones!" he thundered,
   "How we might make them blunder!
      Put your minds to wonder
    To bring them here in greater number
       To our igneous ship asunder!"

First did approach one trembling
   And not free
      And spoke to him of volcanic fury
        Who eats the flesh of bulls.
  "Tell them, sire,
      'There is no devil.'"

"Dunce!" in fiery breath spewed out
   From the mouth of him who only shouts.
     "Tried and true
       And many with this lie have died
        And we have fried!"
    "Fool! Away!
      That heat might excite thy imagination
       From my ignescent majesty!"

Another less brave than the first
   Approached him of ignis fatuus
     With great thirst
  And said to him who does not hear
    To whom none are dear
      Or draw near.

"Prince of thieves and tribal lord
  Behold the sword
    Of pride shall make them swell.
  Amputate them from their Maker
    Tell them there is no hell."

"Ignoramus!" said he
  Who had nailed upon the Tree
    He who is Love.
  "Think you not how tried and true
    The chosen few
      We have ensnared with this fare!"
  "Away beast to a cage
    Of torment and rage
      And in agony stew!"

At last a third
  With no sense
    Approached him who does not bend or yield
  To any sword or shield
    Of faith or hope.

"Tempt them, king of sin
  And to this eternal bin
    Cast them in hate.
  Now tell them in song and rhyme this slime:
    'There is still plenty of time.'"

23

We–They

Human beings, it seems, are always looking for a We–They scenario. We seem to derive a sense of our individual and group identity by defining ourselves in contradistinction to another person or group we downgrade as inferior in some way. We feel better about who we are when we are not like those we differentiate ourselves from, ostracize, vilify, and sometimes demonize. We sense our place in the world is more secure if we are a part of something much larger than ourselves, and whatever we are, we are not Them. Rejection follows from this worldview.

It is as if we need to feel superior to someone or something, that humility is not a part of our calculus by nature. We have grouped ourselves throughout history into tribes, clans, villages, towns, city-states, kingdoms, empires, and nations. If we are not fighting a war against Them, then we are on a team or fans of one, or members of a political party, and we define ourselves in part by not being the other team or party. We form cliques, clubs, communities, groups, and circles, all in an effort to gain a sense of belonging, to fulfill our fundamental human need for safety and security, and to define ourselves by what we are not—Them. There is strength and identity in numbers.

At the root of all of this is the foundational principle of all history—the conflict between good and evil. Also at the root is the binary nature of our spontaneous, interior movements toward good and evil and our volitional acts that follow. A problem arises when our understanding of good and evil is erroneous, or we fail to choose the true good even if we know what it is.

The horizontal We–They paradigm in secular society corresponds with the vertical I–Thou of religion in which we look up toward God as the supreme Thou. In the We–They scenario, we view other humans as *other* or sometimes *totally other*. There is often a sense of exclusion and rejection that accompanies the We–They, just as there is a sense of awe and wonder that accompanies the I–Thou. God is seen as the incomprehensible Supreme Being, Supremely Other, and Totally Otherness.

The We–They paradigm also applies in religion just as it does in secular society. This has historically taken the form in Christianity as a Church–World paradigm, where everyone who is not a member of the Church is by definition a member of the World. This paradigm is also understood in terms of Sacred–Secular or Holy–Profane. There is something of the *otherness* about the World, as if there is little but religion to unite us. It is strange, foreign, and filled with potential and actual enemies. This *otherness* has its roots in and is reinforced by the New Testament writings and the writings of early Christian evangelists and theologians, but it had a reality and meaning for them that we in the twenty-first century do not experience. A passage from a sermon by Saint Cyprian, a bishop of Carthage who lived during the third century and is recognized as a Church Father, exemplifies this attitude:

> The world hates Christians, so why give your love to it instead of following Christ, who loves you and has redeemed you? John is most urgent in his epistle when he tells us not to love the world by yielding to sensual desires. Never give your love to the world, he warns, or to anything in it. *A man cannot love the Father and love the world at the same time. All that the world offers is the lust of the flesh, the lust of the eyes and earthly ambition. The world and its allurements will pass away, but the man who has done the will of God shall live forever.*[6]

Such a view in the modern world defies reason when we consider that the Church has always been in the world and the world has always been in the Church. Moreover, the world has not always been evil, and there is much good in the world, while the Church has not always been good, and there is evil in the Church. There is no separating the two, and this seems to be the

---

[6] "Friday of the Thirty-Fourth Week in Ordinary Time," Office of Readings, *The Liturgy of the Hours,* vol. 4, (New York: Catholic Book Publishing Company, 1975), 604.

way God wants it. Christ was sent into the world, not to condemn it, but to save it (John 3:17).

It is inevitable that human beings form We—They and I—Thou paradigms and to advocate eliminating them would be futile. Perhaps it is because they are rooted in human nature, or maybe they arise because of the fallenness of our world and the fundamental and ancient conflict between good and evil. We need a psychological and spiritual distinguishing mechanism even if that mechanism by itself cannot arrive at the true good. Intellect and reason are necessary for that to occur.

I would like to suggest here a more advantageous way of employing the distinguishing mechanism of We—They paradigms. We should resist the temptation of allowing creed, race, color, class, profession, culture, or any other related characteristic to be the basis of the We—They paradigms we will inevitably form. We will naturally gravitate toward those who are similar to us, but it seems to me that when people of good will meet, all distinguishing characteristics recede and concord generally prevails. The reverse is true of people of ill will, or will eventually be so, even if they are tied by the closest of bonds and share social commonalities. Our ultimate We—They paradigm as Christians should be between people of good will (We) and those of ill will (They).

When it comes to God, the most important distinguishing feature in society is Good Will—Ill Will. We find God wherever we find people of good will, and we experience the absence of God in people of ill will. The greatest of all evils is the absence of

God, and the state in which the absence of God is experienced in its fullness is hell.

We are called as Christians to be leaven of good will at home and in society, and to foster a Christian culture so that Christ can be found more easily in the world. Good will and Christian culture can be found in every age, even among people who do not profess to be Christian. This is because Christ is at all times working to save souls, not just during his earthly life, but through his Holy Spirit and through those in every time and place who hear his word in their heart (Romans 2:12–16).

As we redefine our basic We—They paradigm to People of Good Will—People of Ill Will, we may also consider revising our Church—World paradigm to Christian Culture—Non-Christian Culture. We will find these apply to our social interactions in the world as well as within the Church, and that a Christian culture can be found in the world just as a non-Christian culture can be found within the Church.

~

And the central message of this book and all of the books of this series is this: If you feel inspired to live your life more fully for God and walk the path of holiness, know that you do not have to be a hero-saint like Joan of Arc who was burned at the stake after being handed over to her enemies by her own countrymen. Nor do you have to be Thomas More who was beheaded for his faith by the king he served. Nor do you have to be Jesus of

Nazareth who was crucified by the religious leaders of his day after they had given him over to a foreign occupier, and you do not have to be Maximilian Kolbe who sacrificed his life so that another man might preserve his. You do not have to be a missionary or a minister of any kind, and you might not even be called to leave your own home and the life you are now living.

But you do have to show good will. And you do have to obey the Golden Rule and live according to the two Great Commandments of love.

The distinguishing mark of a saint is the practice of good will. All saints have this in common regardless of their personal and historical circumstances. They practiced good will especially when they were confronted with ill will, and the more good will they showed and the more ill will they faced, the more heroic their charity. Heroic charity, the essential requirement of a candidate for sainthood, is the practice of good will in the face of ill will to a heroic degree. The greater the heroic charity, the greater the saint.

Good will is the pen in which every saint's story is written, and the pen God uses to write his will in our lives is the pen of grace.

Do you believe in miracles?

Do you believe in good will?

Do you want to walk the path of holiness?

Do you want to become a saint?

Then when storm clouds are menacing
And closing in all around you
And the heavens are about to burst
And the tempest threatens impending doom
Know that for you the sun is shining
Do not think first to ask him to take it away
Ask him instead to help you through it
For storms can be gifts in disguise
And you need to trust
And practice Himalaya faith
Faith as tall and as wide as a mountain
But even if your faith
Is only as large as a mustard seed
Know that it is enough
Because it is not the size of the gift
That he is looking for
And a mite was all the widow had
Ask with faith and your plea will be heard
And your prayers will be answered
And your faith will save you
And all will be well

And when you look back on your final day
   At the hour when you go to see him
      You will remember the storms
    And you will remember his Love
       And you will know that you were always
      In the Hand of God

24

A Primer on the Spiritual Life, Part 6

When it comes to final judgment, there is nothing more important in life than relationships, especially our relationship with God. The study of human relationships, like the study of love, is both a science and an art. In this section, I will discuss the difference between contrition and forgiveness on one hand, and repentance and reconciliation on the other.

It says in the Gospel that we are to forgive seventy times seven (Matthew 18:21–22). Our Lord was very clear that forgiveness is mandatory (Matthew 6:15), but he also advised that we may shun unrepentant sinners as a final recourse (Matthew 18:15–17). How do we set these two seemingly contradictory precepts in harmony with one another?

Although we are bound to forgive every time a person expresses contrition, we are not required to reconcile with them if they do not show repentance. Contrition is not the same as repentance. Contrition is a *feeling* of sorrow or remorse. Repentance involves an *active effort* to cease doing wrong. There are people who express sorrow but then continue to do wrong. We are not required to reconcile with these people and are perfectly justified in setting physical, psychological, and social boundaries as long as we have taken reasonable measures to correct the wrongdoer and bring him or her to repentance.

There is nothing unchristian or uncharitable about setting boundaries. Progress in the spiritual life depends on learning how to practice a proper love of self, and the proper love of self sometimes requires setting boundaries. Even if a wrongdoer committed one serious sin against us and showed no sign of repentance, we are permitted to set boundaries to ensure that it does not happen again. Just as there are wounds that time will not heal and wounds that God's grace will not fully heal in this life, there are also relationships that are permanently damaged and cannot be repaired through human effort alone. Some differences are irreconcilable and only God's intervention and grace can bring authentic reconciliation.

Reconciliation is less an event that occurs in a moment of time and more of a process and project as are most things in life. There are times when we are better off leaving the other person to God and the work of time and grace, and we may hope that in due course the wheat of conversion and repentance will be sifted from the chaff of sloth and self-complacency.

Reconciliation might not be possible if:

- No attempt to mitigate or repair
- No contrition or sorrow
- No repentance or conversion
- Shared antipathy / mutual dislike
- Antagonism
- Mutual distrust
- Mutual disgust

In difficult relationships when all else fails we may always in good conscience practice silence and disassociation. If virtue is nothing more than well-directed love as Saint Faustina wrote, then sometimes the best form of love is silence, just as Jesus practiced silence at his trial before members of the Sanhedrin. According to Saint Augustine, love is to will the good of another, but willing the good for people of implacable ill will does not mean we have to speak to them or associate with them. Love, according to 1 Corinthians 13, is patient and kind, not jealous or boastful, arrogant or rude (v. 4–5), and according to Luke 10, love is the Good Samaritan (v. 29–37). If a sinner is in dire need, we should offer that person assistance, but we do not have to offer that person social rewards. New Testament love does not demand reconciliation when it comes to people who simply will not repent.

It is also important to know that a person of good cheer is not necessarily a person of good will. New Testament love is much more than affection or mere feeling or emotion. We reveal ourselves through our actions. Even sinners can show affection when they want to manipulate or deceive others. True love is tested in adversity, and it is in adversity that we reveal our true character. People who show affective love but fail to show effective love, or New Testament love, should be treated with a certain reserve and we are permitted to set boundaries and refuse reconciliation with them if they continue a habit of wrongdoing. An appropriate love of self requires that we recognize "frenemies" and "gift horses."

When it comes to enemies, Christian revenge is forgiveness, it is success in the moral and spiritual life, and according to George Herbert, the best revenge is a life well lived ... but that does not mean we have to reconcile with our enemies if they refuse to repent. If we can do no other good, we may patiently endure them and allow evil to exhaust itself.

This moment, too, shall pass.

**Sometimes the Golden Rule is patiently enduring
sinners in silence and disassociation:**

- Do unto others as you would have them do unto you
- Do not do to others what you yourself dislike
- Treat other people as you would like to be treated
- When all else fails, leave that person to God
  (the final solution)

25

The God of Second Chances

If you have done wrong, and even a lifetime of wrong, and want a second chance with someone or some group of people, then know that you always have one that nobody in time or eternity can take away from you. God always gives the present moment, and we may always observe the Golden Rule and obey the two Great Commandments of love of God and neighbor. It is always within our power to be on our best behavior, to put our best foot forward according to our capacity. We may always speak the truth judiciously with love, be reasonable, cooperate with the good intentions of others, show respect, practice good will, be humble and not arrogant, and most of all, trust in the God of Second Chances.

It may take a lifetime, but what is this short life compared to the infinite eras and epochs and ages that await us in eternity? Nothing in this life is definitive, consummate, absolute, or conclusive until God wills it to be.

The Ladder of Relationships

The most important priority in life is relationships

Left	Ladder	Right
Christian and adult behavior	Friendship with God	High standard of moral and social interaction
Christian companionship New Testament saints	Humility	Intellectual virtue Moral virtue Social virtue
Collegial acquaintances and associates	Charity	Mutual assistance and support
Good terms Fraternal rapport Positive regard	Virtue	Bonds of affection, trust, and respect
Intellectual and moral faults	Narcissism	Normal, decent, intelligent, and worthwhile
Trespass and transgression	Vice	Speaking terms
Patience Forbearance Silence Disassociation	Malice	Selfish and arrogant behavior
Stranger, alien, foe, and foreigner	Sin	Evil exposed is evil deposed
	Demonic Diabolic Hell	The Land of Desolation
		The point of no return

It is impossible to reconcile with implacable hatred

26

A Primer on the Spiritual Life, Part 7

Saint Benedict advises his monks in *The Rule of Saint Benedict* to keep death daily before their eyes (*RB* 4). This daily awareness of death is not the same as a morbid fascination or a gloomy foreboding of it, but a spiritual discipline founded on the proper love of self. In the same manner, Saint Alphonsus Liguori's *Preparation for Death* is not meant to foster a pessimistic attitude, although he wrote in the eighteenth century and contemporary readers might have difficulty with his mode of expression.

Eschatology (Gr. *eschaton*, final or last) is a subject area in spirituality that has two meanings:

1. The end times, or the final coming of Christ
2. The final four things: death, judgment, heaven, and hell.

The eschaton is a reality most people would care to forget or overlook, but the proper love of self requires that we make some effort to prepare for the most important day of our lives—the day we pass from this world into eternity.

Saint John of the Cross taught that we will be examined in love at our judgment, and part of that examination will be to determine how well we attended to our spiritual life. Will our priorities in life have been God's love, God's will, and God's glory, or self-love, self-will, and self-glory? The "play now, pay later" approach to life could be costly, and the bill will soon come due. At final judgment, the truth about our lives will be revealed before Truth itself. There will be no argument, no debate, and perhaps not even a discussion. We will see ourselves as we truly are, not as we want to see ourselves, but the way God sees us, and the consequences will be profound. One day of suffering in the next life will make us forget all the enjoyment we experienced on earth. Many people spend most of their adult life preparing for retirement but do not keep death daily before their eyes. The proper love of self obliges us to prepare for death.

Scripture teaches that the human heart is a mystery, and spiritual masters teach that we do not always know what lies deep within our heart. We should not assume that at final judgment our rational intellect will be operative in the same way it is during our mortal life. Psychology has discovered that there is a hidden observer in each of us that watches all we do and remembers everything. The spiritual life teaches that we have a conscience, and we do not know how our conscience and soul will operate when we are separated from the body and appear at judgment.

In the spiritual life, we refer to conscience as the deepest core of our being, the place where we commune with God. Perhaps conscience and the hidden observer are the same faculty, but it is certain that there is a part of the human person where memories are stored and morally evaluated long after we have forgotten them with our conscious mind. No memory is truly effaced or forgotten and we never truly walk away from our misdeeds despite human forgetfulness and the defense mechanisms we use to avoid dealing with them: repression, projection, denial, evasion, etc. Misdeeds can distort our judgment and desires, and even if we are deeply reflective and meditative, we still may not know all that lies within us, including our deepest desires. Being unprepared for death is dangerous. One of the most important principles in the spiritual life is:

> **Spiritual Principle #18**: You always get what you want when it comes to God.

Are we truly aware of the desires that lie deep within our heart? Do we really know what is at the core of our tortuous heart? Yet there are other spiritual principles that counterbalance the mystery of our inner nature:

> **Spiritual Principle #19**: God rewards for effort and not success.

> **Spiritual Principle #20**: There is nothing impossible for God.

Keeping death daily before our eyes and recognizing the mysterious nature of our inner being and the fact that we have done wrong should not lead to a loss of hope. God did not create us for death and nothing is impossible for him. He desires effort more than success. It is up to God to get the train to the station, but we have to lay the track. Our effort in Christian discipleship is symbolic of our desire to correspond with God's plan for our life and be saved.

One of the desert fathers in the monastic tradition taught that everything we do in life is symbolic of how highly we value our relationship with God and how much we want to be saved.

> **Spiritual Principle #21**: Everything in this life is a symbol.

As a framework for personal meditation and as a way to keep death before our eyes in preparation for judgment, I offer nine Sacred Concerns to reflect upon. These will surely matter at the hour of death:

The Nine Sacred Concerns of the Human Person

Person	Who someone truly is before God; moral character, personality, and competencies
Name	One's reputation based on his or her interior acts and exterior deeds in life
Life	All that is seen about a person's life by God and the soul at judgment
Mission	A special task or assignment granted to some but not all

Vocation	The universal call to holiness; one's individual and particular calling in life
Relation	How one related to and served others during this life
Devotion	How one related to and served God during this life
Formation	How a person was shaped and molded throughout his or her life
Integrity	Holiness, saintliness, degree of purification, moral and spiritual perfection, etc.

The nine sacred concerns serve as criteria for reflecting upon how much glory and honor we expect to receive for all eternity. The more we cooperate with God's plan and show good will, the greater will be our reputation for all eternity, the more glory we will deserve, and the more honor will be shown to us. According to the teachings of the saints and Christian spiritual masters, there is nothing selfish about such considerations.

Yet if our eternal glory is important, then God's glory is infinitely more important. All creation exists first and foremost to manifest God's glory.

> **Spiritual Principle #22**: God's glory is the central and unifying principle of all creation.

God's glory refers to how he will be known for all eternity. This may sound self-centered of God—which would be to say

God-centered—but according to Saint Irenaeus, God's glory is that human beings should have life to its fullness. *To live* or *to have life* in this context means not only to have temporal life, but to share in God's divine life and nature (holiness) as well as in his beatitude for all eternity (glory). Thus, God's glory is actually our temporal and eternal good and he is glorified when we are brought to spiritual perfection.

I will close this portion of the primer with two quotes from Julian of Norwich that speak to the unfathomable mercy of God:

> **Spiritual Principle #23**: In eternity, sin is naught.

> **Spiritual Principle #24**: All will be well, all manner of things will be well.

27

Treasures and Pearls

In the Gospel of Matthew we read two of the most reassuring verses in all of Scripture:

> The kingdom of heaven is like a treasure buried in a field, which a person finds and hides again, and out of joy goes and sells all that he has and buys that field. Again, the kingdom of heaven is like a merchant searching for fine pearls. When he finds a pearl of great price, he goes and sells all that he has and buys it. (Matthew 13:44–46)

The pearl in this passage was not hidden as the treasure was, but found by the merchant who was looking for fine pearls. In the ancient Mediterranean world of Jesus' day, the pearl was considered as precious as diamonds and other rare and valuable gemstones are to us today. Its value was not merely in its monetary cost, but it was also highly prized for its beauty and splendor. A pearl was for ancient Mediterranean people what we would today consider "as good as gold" or the "gold standard." It was of inestimable value.

Unlike the pearl, the treasure was purposely hidden, buried as were many treasures in the ancient world to protect them from thieves and roving armies. Unlike the merchant who was looking for pearls, the plowman found the treasure by accident. Both are metaphors for ways people find God. The plowman symbolizes those who do not purposely seek the Kingdom of Heaven and live like there is no death, judgment, heaven, or hell. Yet God has a plan for them, and he can send graces which may or may not look like treasures at the time but are later recognized as godsends. Toil, loss, failure, and even catastrophic events may at the end of our lives be more valuable to our eternal good than wealth, victories, and success. God can also send pleasant treasures like friendships, an ideal job, a mission or vocation, or some other valued good. Treasures come in all varieties, and whatever we need, God sends.

The merchant, on the other hand, found the pearl after a proactive search. He represents those who live with their end in mind and are looking for the Kingdom of Heaven. But whether we are merchant or plowman—and we may have been both at different times in our lives—we acknowledge that God has a plan for every person. The plowman was destined to find the treasure of the Kingdom of Heaven—it did not happen entirely by accident, but by providence. The merchant did not find the pearl merely through his own activity, but with God's help. He was destined to find the pearl of the Kingdom of Heaven. In both cases, there was a certain union of wills. The plowman willed to have the treasure once he found it, just as God willed him to find and have it. The merchant willed to purchase the pearl once he discovered it, just as God willed him to purchase it. Each arrived at their God-given destinies in their own way.

It is sometimes said that "love is nothing more than enlightened self-interest." There was no greater self-interest for the plowman than to have found that treasure, and there was no greater self-interest for the merchant than to have purchased that pearl, yet the greatest self-interest we can have here below is to seek God and the Kingdom of Heaven. Saint Paul says: "Think of what is above, not of what is on earth" (Colossians 3:2). He does not mean that we should disregard our temporal responsibilities or neglect our earthly gifts, but that we should direct ourselves toward our ultimate treasure and pearl. "For where your treasure is, there also will your heart be" (Matthew 6:21).

The Kingdom of Heaven deserves and demands a single-minded response, not at the expense of neglecting our duties of state or earthly responsibilities, but ordering it all to our final goal and destination. This calls for self-sacrifice and detachment. The plowman and merchant had to make sacrifices in order to gain the treasure and pearl, yet sacrifice and detachment are not stressed in the parable. What is emphasized is the value of the object gained (the true good) and a delight in possessing it.

> What eye has not seen, and ear has not heard, and what has not entered the human heart, what God has prepared for those who love him. (1 Corinthians 2:9)

Treasures and Pearls

Conclusion

In the reflections entitled "Christianity in Decline" and "Five Suggestions," I discussed the decline in membership in the Christian Churches of the West and ways this decline could be slowed, halted, or reversed.

In the Catholic world, we speak of and look forward to a New Evangelization. This term has been with us for some time. The Second Vatican Council (1962–1965) focused on, among other topics, the rapid secularization and de-Christianization of the modern world and featured the word *evangelization* throughout its documents. Ten years later, Pope Paul VI published the apostolic exhortation, "Evangelization in the Modern World" (1975), in which he called Catholics to evangelize to those to whom the Gospel has never been preached, and baptized Christians who no longer practice their faith.

In 1978, Pope John Paul II was elected to the papacy and prioritized evangelization as a focus of his pontificate. In a speech at a bishop's conference in Haiti, he called for a "New Evangelization, new in its ardor, methods, and expression," and in "Mission of the Redeemer" (1990), he wrote: "I sense that the moment has come to commit all of the Church's energies to a new evangelization." He also added a third group to Pope Paul VI's two mentioned above: the baptized who have fervor in their faith.

Benedict XVI added the final piece in this short narrative when he wrote that the new evangelization will not be new in its content, that there will be no changes to established doctrine, only innovations and adjustments in its presentation.

Perhaps the new evangelization will gradually materialize over time, but it certainly has not burst onto the scene just yet. To be fair, the Catholic Church has stressed that there is no single formula (Pope Benedict XVI), so the New Evangelization is seemingly something that will have to be worked out by many individuals over time. The current version of the *Catechism of the Catholic Church* became available in the 1990s, and in my humble opinion, it is truth spoken with beauty.

With regard to the reflections entitled "Christianity in Decline" and "Five Suggestions," it should be noted that a decline in church attendance does not precisely equate with a decline in Christianity. There are people who do not attend liturgy or church services but nevertheless pray, believe in God, and live their lives according to Christian faith and morals. They consider themselves Christian and should be counted as such, so maybe we should add a fourth group to the three mentioned above: baptized Christians who do not go to church but otherwise live according to Christian faith and morals. These people, too, are in need of evangelization.

The problem of disconnect between the Church and the world with regard to history and knowledge and the cultural dissonance that ensues from it cannot be overestimated. How to bridge that gap is the main challenge Christianity will face during the twenty-first century and probably beyond. Anyone who undertakes ministry will be tasked with this challenge, and some kind of innovation should be expected. A Hero Is Chosen series is an attempt at innovation, and whoever said that the New Evangelization was strictly limited to preaching from the pulpit?

Afterword

In the Introduction I said that every book is something of a journey, and the journey of this book is a metaphor for the journey we take through life. This book's journey began on the front cover and ends with the final illustration on the following page. "Desert Footprints" represents the fulfillment of the monk's journey. We do not know how the monk fared, and we are not sure how our journey will end either. We have only one terrestrial life throughout all of eternity, and this book was written to inspire us to consider how we are spending it. Once the journey of this life ends, it will be over forever.

I will close with this thought:

The most beautiful word in any language is *yes*. When we say yes to God, we give him a treasure. If life is God's greatest gift, and we give our lives to him to do with as he wills, then we give to God his greatest gift to us.

I hope you consider this as you turn the page, many of you for the last time.

About the Author

Brother Emmanuel Labrise, O.S.B., received a B.S. from Saint Vincent College, an M.A. from Bowling Green State University, and an M.A. from Notre Dame Seminary. A contemplative monk with over twenty years' experience in monastic life, he spent six years as a member of the Order of Carthusians and has been a monk in the Order of Saint Benedict since 2009. Among other assignments, he has taught in a seminary college, worked in a seminary formation program, and given conferences at a retreat house. He is currently living the eremitical life in which his main activities are prayer, reading, reflection, and writing.

Books by Brother Emmanuel Labrise, O.S.B.
A Hero Is Chosen Series
Hero Stories of the Saints

Book One: *Reflections of an Uncommon Monk: Toward a Theology of Hero-Sainthood*
Serves as an introduction to the series and its spiritual and moral foundation

Book Two: *Mission of the Maiden: The Hero Story of Joan of Arc*

    Part One: Historical Context
Fourteenth- and fifteenth-century medieval Europe; High Middle Ages; Hundred Years' War; history of France and England

    Part Two: Mission of the Maiden
Joan's hero-saint story focusing on her public mission (hero-event) from the time she left Domrémy until her interrogation, trial, and burning at the stake (hero-moment)

Book Three: *God's Good Servant and the King's: The Hero Story of Thomas More*

    Part One: Historical Context
Fifteenth- and sixteenth-century Renaissance Europe; Reformation period; English and Church history

    Part Two: God's Good Servant and the King's
Thomas More's hero-saint story focusing on his public dissent from King Henry VIII (hero-event) until his execution (hero-moment)

Many years ago, a little donkey lived in a small town near Bethany. He dreamed of going places and of being strong and useful, but he could be none of those things because he was tied to a post by the fence. A friendly girl assured him that God must have a very special purpose for him, but the little donkey wondered whether this was so. One day, two men came and told his owner that he was needed. Has the little donkey's time finally come?

Notes and Personal Reflections:

Notes and Personal Reflections: